NOW WE ARE HERE, WHERE ON EARTH ARE WE?

Also by Sheila Bridge

Are We Nearly There Yet?
The Art of Imperfect Parenting
The Art of Plate Spinning

Now We Are Here, Where On Earth Are We?

A year in the life of an almost functional family

Sheila Bridge

Hodder & Stoughton

LONDON   SYDNEY   AUCKLAND

Typeset by Palimpsest Book Production Limited,
Polmont, Stirlingshire
Printed and bound in Great Britain by
Clays Ltd, St Ives plc.

Hodder and Stoughton Ltd
A Division of Hodder Headline PLC
338 Euston Road
London NW1 3BH

Wednesday, 1 January

'We will be landing in a few moments. Please fasten your seat belts, ensure your chairs are in the upright position and extinguish all cigarettes. We hope you have enjoyed your flight and look forward to your company again. Meanwhile we wish you a safe onward journey and a prosperous New Year.'

It was my voice over the loudspeaker. I was flying a plane-load of strangers into some obscure location. The plane banked steeply and I prepared for our final approach. Suddenly I found myself struggling with the controls; the descent was steeper than I'd expected, the plane seemed to be out of control, the landing was going to be bumpy.

'Emergency landing procedures, cabin attendants to the doors, please,' I just managed to announce before bracing myself for touchdown. The runway flashed past. I blanked out momentarily and came round to find we were slowing down and the crisis had past.

'That was a close one.'

My co-pilot wasn't listening, craning his head to look out of the window. He eventually turned round and shouted at me, 'You idiot! You've brought us to the wrong place. WHERE ON EARTH ARE WE?'

I woke with a jolt and discovered to my considerable relief that I was not in fact lost on an obscure island in the Atlantic with an angry plane-load of passengers but safely sharing a very small bed in my mother's spare room with my husband David. I rolled over to check the time: 5.00 a.m. David was sleeping soundly and Emma and Matthew were warmly tucked up in makeshift beds on the floor. Even the dog was snoring gently somewhere under the bed. All was well.

Relaxing into the relief of simply being Mummy again, I pondered on my nonsensical nightmare. Too much late-night cheese and wine? Or did my navigational crisis perhaps have a deeper significance?

It wasn't difficult to sort out the elements that had surfaced from my subconscious and come to life in my dream. First there was the fact of the journey itself. Lying in bed early on New Year's Day, I was obviously not on a literal journey, but for the last few months I have been on a metaphorical journey. We are in the process of moving, moving between one job and the next, between our old home and our new one. David has been tentatively offered a new job in the north and we are waiting for the formal interview at the end of January before the offer is confirmed. I am finding the middle of a long decision-making process an uncomfortable place to be. Personally I would like to start the New Year knowing where I'm going and when I'm going to get there, which probably explains why someone who has never driven anything larger than a family estate should take the controls of a passenger jet plane in her dreams! I do like being in control, it's one of my biggest spiritual hang-ups. The trouble is that when you insist on being in control there's no one else to blame when you mess up. And landing at the wrong airport is a pretty good metaphor for messing up badly. But dreams can be confusing: should I seek counselling for my deep-rooted fear of getting lost or sign up for flying lessons?

I know I have been worrying about what would happen to us if we misread the directions into our future. What if we end up living in the wrong place? What if moving the children affects them disastrously? What if we never make any friends again? What if they all wear flat caps and say 'ecky thump' (whatever that means)? These are the fears that have been swimming below the surface of my life.

I sighed and rolled over. Why, when I have spent the last two years deciding to do a two-year Reader-ship training course which I have only just started, do we have to move? Why, when I am so entrenched in our community, so involved at church, do we have to move? Why, when we have finally got the house the way we wanted it, do we have to move? These were questions to which there were no answers, except the fact that north had become the one direction in which we were being inexorably moved.

We had told David's mother as much over Christmas. She has been so preoccupied with moving house herself for the last few months that we hadn't wanted to mention it before. She is about to move a remarkable three hundred yards down the road, to her third house in the same two streets where she has spent most of her life. If Dave and I do move this year it will be the sixth time in the twelve years we have been married. And it will be the twelfth time I will have relocated in my life. As I'm only thirty-four, that's an average of a new location every three years. With my father's job, I moved countries and continents regularly throughout my childhood and I'm sure one of the things that attracted me to David when I first met him was the fact that he'd spent his whole life in the same place. It seemed such a novel idea to me.

The irony is that now, at this mid-life point, I have finally been cured of 'itchy feet syndrome'. A couple of years ago, I actually wanted to move; I couldn't understand why we were still hanging around, why I couldn't walk away from difficult relationships and potentially draining situations. But I'd come through that feeling and now I've really learnt to belong, to love through thick and thin. I've made the kind of friendships that I figured would see me into my dotage. Why (I wondered for the fourth time in a few minutes), when I've finally reached such a point of contentment and commitment, do we have to move?

Still no answer.

The dog woke up, stretched and licked Matthew's face. Fortunately Matthew is besotted with the dog and can think of no more wonderful way to wake up. Their mutual delight in each other and in the new day that had dawned did something to lift my spirits.

'Happy New Year, Matthew,' I whispered over David, who was still sleeping. 'Do you want to take Chester out into Grandma's garden?'

Chester is only a puppy and still has a small and unreliable bladder. Matthew was amazingly keen on the prospect of a cold early morning walk in his pyjamas, but this shouldn't have surprised me. Matthew is just keen, period.

I slid down under the covers for five more minutes of peace and warmth but didn't even have time to get comfortable before small boy and dog returned, salivating with excitement.

'It's snowing, it's snowing!' Matthew shouted with joy, waking both his dad and his sister in the process.

'Oh no,' were David's first words of the new year. Emma was a tad more positive.

'Can we have a snowball fight?'

'Yes, Emma, *you* may,' I replied, 'but the real question is "Can we get up the drive?"' Grandma's house is at the end of a very long, very steep drive. We were expected at my sister's for lunch and the prospect of pushing a well-packed car up several hundred yards of snowy incline to the main road didn't fire me with enthusiasm. Staying in bed seemed a more attractive option.

But David was already up and dressed. Galvanised by the thought of being snowed in with his in-laws, he set about collecting shovels, old towels, doormats and frayed pieces of matting from the back of the garage. At no point in our progress up the drive did he give way to optimism, making gloomy predictions about being snowed in for days all the way to the main road. In spite of this, twenty sweaty minutes later, we made it. We even reached my sister's by lunchtime.

Our visit there would have been a success had it not been for Chester, who disgraced himself: he peed on the carpet, snarled at my nephew and left teeth-marks in my brother's new shoes. I spent the whole afternoon alternately apologising for his appalling behaviour and inwardly worrying about his dominant personality. He's not even as high as the average pair of knees but he swaggers around

'At no point in our progress up the drive
did he give way to optimism'

people's ankles with all the confidence of a dog three times his size.

The afternoon confirmed two of my three New Year resolutions: one, 'Train the dog' (but don't rule out surgical intervention); two, 'Read more' (I borrowed several books from my sister). I failed with number three, 'Eat less', but then it was a delicious lunch.

On the way home I dipped into one of my own books, *My Utmost for His Highest* by Oswald Chambers. It's a devotional classic that I was given the Christmas before last and I'm ashamed to admit that this is my second attempt at the January readings. Today I read, 'Where people will not take God seriously, anxiety and superstition will flourish.' I can testify to the anxiety part, dreams about piloting lost aeroplanes are evidence enough for that, but I haven't yet given way to superstition or star-gazing. As fearful as I am about the future, I have to admit that God has guided us safely through the past and I have no reason to think he'll abandon us now.

A lovely winter sunset crowned our journey home.

'It's going to be a lovely day tomorrow,' Matthew informed us from the back seat of the car.

'Why's that, then?' I asked him.

'It's easy,' he said, 'Red sky at night . . . Angel Delight!'

I'm not quite sure what milk puddings have got to do with it, but for those who follow their Father in faith, the outlook has got to be good.

Saturday, 4 January

David and Emma have been away overnight. Yesterday was moving day for his mum and they went to lend a hand. After four months of stress and hassle with the move being on, then off, then on again, she managed to move out twenty-seven years to the exact day she moved in. This remarkable coincidence seemed more of a reassuring 'God-incidence' and everything went well on the day.

When she was with us over Christmas, I tried to prepare her for the discomfort and inconvenience of moving day (Gran is not used to roughing it). As a seasoned mover myself, I gently suggested to her that it would be perfectly acceptable for everyone concerned if she were to send David out to fetch fish and chips for supper on the big day. She had given me a horrified look and informed me that she had already booked a table at the local French restaurant!

Sure enough, I rang last night and the curtains were already up at the windows, the beds were made, the electric blankets were on and everyone was dressing up to go out. You've got to hand it to her, that's moving with style.

David and Emma collected an extra child on the way home today: our godson, who's staying till Monday. Three children for the last three days of the Christmas holidays – 'Was this a good idea?' I ask myself.

Tuesday, 7 January

The first day of term – mother's delight! The extra-child idea worked well; introducing a new playmate at the tedious end of the holidays is an idea worth repeating. It just made for rather a lot of washing and more than the usual amount of mess. I spent a happy morning excavating our home from under what remained of the Christmas decorations.

Met with my Sunday school team last night. None of them know yet that I'm unlikely to be around to lead them for the second half of this year, but it's all so uncertain at the moment there was no point in saying anything. But it was an uncomfortable feeling.

Friday, 10 January

The piano arrived this morning. Gran's piano (not to be misread as Grand piano) now occupies most of one wall in the sitting room. It came at five to eight this morning in a large van with two burly removal men. Gran's removal firm had agreed to store it until they could deliver it to our house on their way to another job. Gran doesn't really have room for it in her smaller house.

I didn't think it would fit through our narrow front door or round the two right-angled bends into the lounge, but the removal men took one look at the route to the back door (along a footpath, down an alleyway and through a garden) and decided that this piano *would* go round corners. It took two cups of tea and five minutes of effort.

After only twenty-four hours as the owner of a piano, I can appreciate the need for piano lessons. Not for me, I'm sorry to say, I gave them up at thirteen due to an intrinsic lack of talent, but for Emma who has inherited Gran's ear for music as well as her piano. She can pick out a tune with ease. Unfortunately at the moment the only tunes she is picking out are Christmas carols, which are wearing a bit thin by this stage in January. But we have already survived the recorder and the violin (surely nothing can be more painful than a seven-year-old's first scrapings on a violin?). Practice makes perfect and she now has a new incentive to practise: she gets paid for it.

This morning I set up an incentive scheme to encourage desirable behaviour. It's not bribery, I prefer to think of it as 'positive reinforcement'. There are now two charts in the kitchen, one labelled 'Emma's Earnings' and the other labelled 'Matthew's Money'. They get 3p increments to their pocket money for every tick on their charts, and deductions for undesirable behaviour are at parental discretion. We'll see how it goes.

The rest of the day was spent preparing for Sunday's family service on Noah. The service theme is 'Faith for a New Start' and what I am preparing to say is all rather too close to home: i.e. how God gives Noah a really wacky plan to follow and how sometimes we are also given instructions for our future that don't appear to make sense. The relevance of this message to our personal situation will be lost on most of the congregation, but it hasn't been lost on me.

Saturday, 11 January

Last night David tried to upgrade the computer. Apparently it needed a larger memory. I wasn't convinced, but then I'm just jealous because I could do with a larger memory myself. I was nervous about David attempting the installation on his own because I really need my computer. The last time David took it apart it developed a fault and had to go to back to the shop to be fixed. This turned into a long-running saga: every time I got it home it wouldn't work, every time I took it back to the shop it would have mysteriously fixed itself, and so on. Other people's experiences have confirmed

12

this phenomenon: a friend of mine has finally got hers back after weeks of problems; hers needed a 'fat agnes' (whatever one of those is), so I suppose I should be grateful we just need more memory. But I'd still prefer it if David didn't do it unaided and on the 'if it ain't broke, don't fix it' principle, I'd rather it wasn't upgraded at all. I made negative noises all day. But it didn't work. Nor did the upgrade.

I took myself upstairs as my computer came to pieces on the dining-room table. It took him all evening to put it back together again. He called me down after eleven for the grand 'switch on'.

The power light came on, the hard drive began to whir and then there was a wisp of grey smoke and the whole thing expired. I bit hard on phrases about a little bit of knowledge being a dangerous thing and stomped off to bed, leaving David to spend over an hour on a lengthy post-mortem. I don't think he slept much for worrying. I wouldn't have minded but January is not the best month for bills. As it is we have to pay for Spring Harvest this month, put some flooring down in the hallway and I'm seriously considering having the dog neutered, so we could do without a hefty repair bill for the computer.

Monday, 13 January

My reading this morning was in Genesis, about God going ahead and preparing situations: Abraham's servant found the right girl for his master's son in a strange country after a long journey. Please, Lord, find us the right place to live and the right school for the children.

On a more mundane note, I've booked the dog in for his op on Wednesday. The vet agreed that his dominant attitude would definitely be improved by the removal of certain parts of his anatomy. Poor thing, I feel a bit sorry for him, but he's already snapped once at the children and once was enough. If I can't trust him with them then he can't stay, so I hope this procedure works.

I collected the computer from the repair place today. The bill wasn't as much as we'd expected and David got his extra memory after all.

Tuesday, 14 January

Met with all the youth leaders from church last night and came away with an acute sense of failure and exhaustion. Woke this morning and realised that both these negative nasties were being held together by the strong glue of resentment. Basically I feel I'm going flat out, achieving very little for no pay and poor appreciation. I allowed myself to drown in this sea of self-pity for as long as it took me to drink my first cup of tea, then I decided I wouldn't do any Sunday school stuff today, I wouldn't do my Readership assignment, I wouldn't even think about next month's family service, instead I'd do my own stuff all day.

It worked. I've had a very satisfying day planning a completely new writing project and it's been an excellent antidote to resentment.

Wednesday, 15 January

Dropped the dog off at the vet's at 8.00 a.m. Dropped the kids with a friend at 8.10 and found ourselves in Scardale by 10.30. David had a business meeting in Scardale with the firm that's offering him the new job so I decided to come along for the ride. I spent the morning wandering around the town that could be our new home. I raided the tourist office, town council and education department for as much information on the area as I could find and retreated to Woolworth's cafe to 'read all about it'. After meeting David for lunch, we drove around several neighbouring areas before heading for home. The whole place was bathed in sunshine but David assured me this wasn't normal. At least we saw it at its best.

On our return the children had been collected from school by yet another friend and when they asked we were somewhat vague about where we'd been all day and why we'd been there. They were more interested in the dog, anyway. We collected him from the vet's at teatime. He looked rather sorry for himself and went straight to hide in a corner when we got him home. After sulking for the best part of an hour, he was finally persuaded to come out by a few choice morsels of tenderly steamed chicken. I hope he forgives us.

After the kids had gone to bed I had time to reflect on my first day in our new location. In fact my reflection only brought all the negative feelings to the surface. I thought about how awful it will be to stand in a school playground full of strangers, how the kids will miss all their friends, how much I'll miss our neighbours, and wondered how quickly our place here would be filled. Deciding to watch *Shadowlands* this evening probably wasn't the best idea, given my maudlin state of mind, but it did at least give me the excuse to bawl my eyes out. One question from the whole sad story summed up my dilemma succinctly: 'Why do we choose to love when we know what pain will be caused when we have to let go of that which we love?'

Sunday, 19 January

The dog is recovering well and doesn't seem too resentful. He's even stopped snarling. He now limits himself to 'swearing' mildly in dog language. As this doesn't involve teeth, I think I can cope.

Friday night was girls' night at the house of a friend. Six of us 'playground' friends try to get together every six weeks or so. It was, as always, a riot of good conversation and general hilarity. I had thought beforehand that I might say something about our move but in the end I couldn't bear to sound a jarring note.

Yesterday afternoon I took the children to see a stage production of *The Lion, the Witch and the Wardrobe*. It's one of our favourite books and we were intrigued to see how it could be adapted for the stage. Being an amateur production it had its weak moments but was pretty good, considering. The story ends with the four children, now kings and queens in Narnia, chasing the white stag through the forest. They are not sure whether to follow, but then one of them boldly declares, 'We should not hang back out of fear or foreboding about what the future may hold.'

As if that wasn't enough, I showed a video in Sunday school this morning. It was the story of Abraham setting out from Ur, and a booming, somewhat Shakespearian voice of 'God' called him to 'uproot from the past, begin afresh, I will take you where you belong'. It sent shivers down my spine.

God seems to favour a multi-media megaphone to get my attention at the moment.

Tuesday, 21 January

I started ringing schools today and asking for

prospectuses. It made me feel that I was doing something at last; it's getting very stressful waiting for David's interview next Monday. At least gathering some information can't do any harm. In the evening I rang the few contacts I've collected. First I tried the auntie of a friend of my friend who lives in Scardale (the auntie lives there, that is, not the friend of my friend, nor my friend!). Trying to explain the complicated link between us and how I came to have her phone number seemed hardly worth the effort, but I tried. I may as well have said, 'Look I'm a complete stranger and I might be moving to Scardale, tell me all you know.' Anyway, she was very sweet and we had quite a helpful conversation. Next I tried a number my mum had given me. (My mother can be guaranteed to know someone who knows someone in just about any location you care to mention. If she met an alien from Mars I'm sure she'd uncover some tenuous connection. 'So you've been to Earth then, I know someone who lives there.') This contact, however, wasn't one of her better ones, the gentleman being very pleasant but rather elderly and hard of hearing. We had a loud but otherwise polite conversation during which he invited us all to tea. Unfortunately he didn't seem to know much about Scardale even though he lives there, so I respectfully declined. I think I've had enough of calling complete strangers.

Thursday, 23 January

I had another vivid dream early this morning. I dreamt I was waking up after surgery on my abdomen. It was weird, I couldn't move and I could even feel the stitches in my tummy. I had a few moments of panic and then I woke up for real. The first thing I did was check my stomach for scars!

I'm not going to think about this dream too deeply, it's probably just a symptom of my inner state of anxiety. Jane and David came round this evening. They have been one of the few couples aware of our job dilemma and we asked them round to pray with us. Our conversation and time of prayer was really helpful. I had described my feelings as being like a log carried along by a fast-flowing stream, getting bumped, bruised and feeling out of control. We listened and prayed for a while, and in the silence I had the reassurance that although I felt I was being swept along I was actually being held in a current, and that current was the love of God. As Andy prayed he shared with us that he felt all the doors would be flung open for us and we ended the evening feeling much better than when we'd started.

Friday, 24 January

Better dreams last night; I dreamt I was at a dinner

party having a great time. Vast improvement on the night before!

My friend Sarah came for lunch today and took one step inside the front door before declaring: 'PHEW! This house smells.' Sniff, Sniff . . . 'Of dog,' she added triumphantly.

Well, why be objectionable when with a little more effort you can be downright rude?

I admit to feeling sensitive about Chester's earlier preference for puddling on the hall carpet, but I'd done my best with the lemon disinfectant and anyway he's been almost house-trained since Christmas, so I wasn't about to apologise for an incontinent dog, especially not when I couldn't smell a thing.

We disputed the matter in the hall for several moments before I led her into the kitchen and offered her a fragrant (to my nose, anyway) bowl of recently cooked basmati rice to smell, whereupon she reluctantly conceded defeat. She doesn't eat rice or even cook it. Hardly surprising, really, neither would I if I thought it smelt of dog!

At least the rice wasn't for lunch, so we parted still friends. I read her a story about smells I'd found in yesterday's paper. Apparently someone's discovered that children working in a floral-scented classroom will add up more accurately than those in less fragrant classrooms. As Sarah home-schools her two daughters I thought she might be interested in my discovery – well, every little helps. It seemed such a simple remedy for being feeble with numbers that I've already put my hyacinths on my desk.

'Not much help if you suffer from hay fever,' she pointed out.

I thought about our conversation after she'd gone and realised that I do indeed expend a lot of time and energy ensuring my personal and household aroma is inoffensive, so it's quite shocking to remind myself that I am meant to 'stink' as a Christian, or be 'the aroma of Christ' as Paul puts it. Attractive to some, offensive to others. It adds a whole new meaning to the idea of getting right up someone's nose.

I'm not sure if I am as spiritually 'pungent' as I should be. I should pluck up the courage to ask someone; perhaps I'll start by asking Sarah.

Saturday, 25 January

Today I went on a retreat day for children's workers and took another member of my Sunday school team with me. The day exceeded all my expectations. I was expecting little pep talks about visual aids, take-home sheets and story-telling. I had expected a day off my own train of thought, which has been exclusively chugging towards David's interview on Monday and the changes it might bring into our lives. But the title of the day should have warned me: 'Surprises on the Way'.

All the sessions were an extended meditation on

the story of Paul's journey to Damascus, the one where he meets the Lord for the first time. The speaker began the day by getting us to think about the metaphor of life being a journey.

'Journeys can be either exciting or daunting, exhausting or stimulating, how we feel when we are faced with new places, unfamiliar landscapes, a change in routine, new people . . .' I couldn't believe my ears! Has this guy been reading my diary for the last month? All that he was saying was so personally relevant I couldn't believe it could also be relevant to everyone else in the room. As we were taken through times of worship and times of silence, I became aware that God had something very particular to say to me.

We followed Saul on his journey as he left Jerusalem, full of purpose and fire, full of self-importance and misdirected zeal. We watched as he was brought low, how his whole world was 'unmade' and then remade. We saw how his grip was forcibly loosened on his status and prestige as he was left blind, helpless, overwhelmed and needing to be led along. We reflected on how such experiences are very much a part of the Christian journey. Saul came into a 'nowhere house, in a nowhere place' under the ministry of a 'nobody', Ananias. Saul's rebirth was in many ways humiliating and he was yet to spend a long time in obscurity before the Lord would use him.

During the first of two periods of private meditation I read Psalm 11 and thought about God being in control. The day's 'journey' theme gave me permission to think through my own journey, and I wrote a long letter to God outlining my fears for myself, my complaints about moving my children around in the way I had been moved as a child, my fears for David, my hopes, my requests. Finally I confessed my feeble trust about the way he was leading us. It helped enormously to have written down everything I wanted to say. Anxiety often creates a kind of 'hiss' in my mind, not unlike interference on the radio, which makes it hard to tune in to what God is saying. Writing it all down reduces that hiss and I went into the next session feeling much better.

The Lord had said enough already; I wasn't expecting him to say any more, but during another time of silence I was suddenly ambushed by a vivid memory that seemed to come out of nowhere. In my mind's eye I pictured a child on a swing. I recognised the garden, the child's dress, the halo of golden curls. The child was me, the swing was in one of our many gardens and I knew I was recalling a moment from my childhood. I wondered why I should suddenly recall such a tiny moment in such detail, and while I wondered I felt the Lord say to me, 'I knew you long before you knew me, I watched over you and protected you through so many moves in your childhood. Don't you think I can do the same for your children?'

It's hard to express the intimacy of this moment. To say I had a lump in my throat seems lame. It felt as if God cuddled me.

In the final private meditation period of the day I read Psalm 32 and the words of verses 8 to 10 stood out of the page:

I will instruct you and teach you in the way
    you should go;
    I will counsel you and watch over you.
Do not be like the horse or the mule,
    which have no understanding
    but must be controlled by bit and bridle
    or they will not come to you.
Many are the woes of the wicked,
    but the LORD's unfailing love
    surrounds the man who trusts in him.

The horse and mule part was a bit of a rebuke but the initial promise was great. I sailed home on air.

Monday, 27 January

Interview day at last. David left early for Scardale.

Tuesday, 28 January

It looks like a green light. David was pleased with

all the details of the job offer and excited by the job itself. But he wasn't the only one with a job offer. I had a call this afternoon accepting the new writing project I submitted two weeks ago. This piece of excellent timing leaves me feeling that David is not the only one with a new direction.

In another piece of good timing I had a letter from a close friend this morning, someone who's been aware of our job decision and had taken the time to pray and write. Rather sheepishly she referred me to Psalm 32:8–10, which she felt was for me, and confessed that she felt somewhat uncomfortable telling a good friend to stop behaving like a mule! Little did she realise how well she had heard from God. She was very relieved when I phoned to tell her that God had already told me I was being a stubborn mule. She also told me that she felt there would be much 'rain' ahead for both of us. Technically I'm sure she's right, given what I already know about the climatic conditions of Scardale, but she took this to mean blessing. I hope she is right because my wellies leak!

Saturday, 1 February

The week has passed in a blur of relief. Relief that the interview is finally over and relief at all the divine reassurance we have received about our decision. We haven't yet received the offer in writing so, technically, we are waiting to dot the i's and cross the t's. But we've already decided that if the job's offered we'll take it.

Meanwhile, today is pay day. Not for us, unfortunately. The kids have been poring over their 'tick' charts calculating their increments. This chart system has been working quite well; on a good week they can double their pocket money, not a bad return on a couple of chores a day. They lost a few this week, though, for bad behaviour and at pay-out time the main perpetrator was suitably repentant. I applied leniency and gave her three undeserved ticks before handing over her week's earnings.

'But I haven't earned that much,' she remarked with surprise.

'I know. Those last three ticks are called forgiveness.'

I prefer carrots to sticks.

Monday, 3 February

Last night we talked about how we might tell the kids about moving. We decided to wait until we have the job offer in hand and then to take them up to see the place as soon as possible after that. The half-term holiday in a couple of weeks' time would give us an ideal opportunity, assuming the job offer comes by then. David could take some time off and we could all go up for a few days together. Even better, I've found out it's not half-term up there so we could even see some schools in action. We hope to try to sell it to them as a fun 'let's explore our new location' experience. Today I checked out Gran's availability to come along with us, as her presence would add to the 'fun' dimension and she'd also be able to look after the children if David and I want to look at schools or houses on our own.

Gran agreed this morning so I started phoning round to find a three-bedroomed holiday cottage, suitable for a dog, a Gran, two children and two grown-ups, preferably with a garden, anywhere near Scardale. This proved to be a tall order. After five or six phone calls to several different tourist information places I was finally given the phone number for what sounded like the ideal place. I rang it all morning and only got an answering service. I gave up.

Tuesday, 4 February

Sarah came for lunch again today. No complaints about nasty odours this time. She is contemplating the purchase of a home computer to enhance her daughters' 'school' sessions, so I let her girls loose on the more educational stuff we've bought for our kids to use on our computer and this gave Sarah and me a rare hour of uninterrupted conversation. Sarah is one of the few friends I have told about the possibility of the new job up north so it was a relief to be able to talk it over with someone. I'm having an uncomfortable time talking with friends who don't yet know. David doesn't want me to tell anyone else until the job offer is confirmed because he thinks the children should be the first to know. I think he's right, but I still feel awkward talking trivia with close friends when all the time there's something so major on my mind. I just hope the letter will come by the weekend and then we can talk to the children and our news will be public.

After our previous disagreement over smells, Sarah brought me a peace-offering: a book called *Life's Little Instruction Book.* It turned out to be a list of 1,028 modern proverbs, handy tips and helpful advice. It's compulsive reading. I've reached number 914 already and am disappointed not to have found one along the lines of 'Never remark on a strange smell in the house of a friend'. Oh well. I did find 'Always put a packet of Wet Wipes in the glove compartment of your car', which made me feel virtuous because I do. Then I found 'Read all the books short-listed for the Booker Prize' and felt miserable because I don't. I don't think I'll bother with the remaining 114. I have enough trouble with lists of my own instructions, let alone anyone else's.

Mrs N. with the holiday cottage still isn't answering her phone or replying to messages.

Thursday, 6 February

Uncertainty has affected our sleep patterns. I get off to sleep okay but wake early, and David can't get to sleep and then can't wake up. This morning he had to catch an early plane and was worried that he wouldn't wake up in time, so he set *two* alarm clocks. The first one woke him instantly and he went off to the bathroom leaving me to roll over and try to go back to sleep. The second alarm only went off when I had succeeded. Not only was it louder, it was also hidden, which meant I had to turn the light on to find it. Busy with his shaver in the bathroom, David didn't hear the thumps and moans in the bedroom as I struggled to assassinate the alarm clock under the bed. I could have thrown it at him when he came in for his jacket and tie.

'Thank you, dear, I'm wide awake now.'

I hope I get an early night tonight to make up for it. Tried the lady in Scardale with the holiday cottage again; still just the answerphone.

Friday, 7 February

I didn't get the early night I'd needed. David did, but I sat up late finishing an assignment for my Readership course. When I did finally get upstairs I crept in as quietly as I could so as not to disturb him.

He waited for a whole ten minutes before asking me, 'Did you turn the oven off?'

Why on earth would such a question occur to him at half eleven at night? 'Tea was six hours ago,' I reassured him, 'of course it's off . . . I think.'

He made a suspiciously incoherent reply.

'Are you asleep?' I asked.

'I'm not sure,' he replied.

He *was* asleep and had been throughout the conversation, but I still lay awake for another ten minutes, wondering whether or not the oven was off, before I eventually got up to check. He denied all knowledge of our conversation this morning.

At least tomorrow is my lie-in. Our system of lie-ins has been one of the sustaining policies of our marriage. It wasn't exactly written into our marriage vows but that wouldn't have been a bad idea ('Wilt thou love her, comfort her . . . and let her sleep as long as she likes on Saturdays?'). The deal is that I get up for the kids, the dog and anyone else who needs me on any night, but I don't appear on Saturday mornings until I feel like it.

Saturday, 8 February

Perversely, I couldn't stay in bed this morning once I'd heard the postman call. I had to come down to see if the job offer had come. It hadn't. Why is it taking so long? I feel as if I've been in a waiting-room all week; even the lady with the holiday cottage is still refusing to answer her phone.

I retreated back to bed with a bad mood and a cup of tea before anyone noticed I was up. At least I found some reassurance in my morning's reading: 'See, I am sending an angel ahead of you to guard you along the way and to bring you to the place I have prepared' (Exodus 23:20). I hope so, Lord, I do hope so.

Evening: At last, the lady with the holiday cottage picked up her messages and rang to say yes, the place was available but, no, it didn't have a garden. Not having a garden will be a bit of a problem with the dog but as it is 'on the edge of the moor' there should be plenty of countryside for walking him. It sounded great, we booked it.

Sunday, 9 February

I'm giving in to the children's every whim at the moment, probably because I am dreading the distress they might feel when we tell them about the move. This afternoon they wanted to bake.

They have always loved baking. I can't think why, all they create is a mess: a mess in a bowl and a mess on the floor, and somewhere along the way my cheerful tone of voice ('Let's do this together, won't it be fun!' à la Joyce Grenfell) is always reduced to

31

a hissed set of exasperated orders: 'Here, let me do it . . . watch what you're doing . . . *don't* step in that.'

Recently Emma has mastered an easy oat biscuit recipe which doesn't require any adult assistance. She simply says, 'Mummy, can I make some biscuits?' and I say, 'Certainly, dear, and I'll have a cup of tea while you are at it.' Bliss. Isn't growing up great?

This afternoon, however, she had more ambitious plans. Yesterday she had disappeared into her room with five huge cookery books, several pads of plain paper and her brother. I knew it would mean trouble but I felt loath to interrupt their flow of creative energy, especially as it kept them quiet for the best part of an hour. They emerged to cries of 'Can we do some baking, Mum?' and presented me with two handwritten 'recipes'.

'It's an S periment,' added Matthew.

I could tell. I didn't know quite how to break it to them that mixing two bags of chocolate chips with three bags of marshmallows, one packet of icing sugar, eight pieces of bread and three pints of milk was very unlikely to produce anything remotely resembling a cake (a cow pat, maybe) but I did at least manage to put off the baking until this afternoon. I also spent a little time teaching them about the chemistry of cooking, adjusted the proportions of their recipes and added some flour, fat and eggs to their list of ingredients. I even persuaded Emma to use oats instead of bread and to add a little golden syrup.

Observing the rearrangements to his sister's recipe, Matthew scribbled through his own and replaced it with 'Take 9 oz of sponge'! Sensible boy, he only really wanted to ice the thing.

So this afternoon I was on hand to assist with both their creations. I stayed amazingly calm as Emma boiled chocolate chips in syrup and ladled in the milk. Her 'Triplely Dumpshous' recipe didn't quite live up to its wonderful name; it came out as a sort of gingerbread/flapjack cross, only without the ginger. Matthew's sponge tasted remarkably like banana bread, which was quite an achievement because I hadn't seen any bananas go into it.

The real fun came later when the cakes had cooled. They slapped on the icing and sherbet pips in a way that would have given a dentist heart failure. When that was done I was left trying to rediscover my work surfaces under puddles of congealed cake mixture and slops of icing. But I felt it had been worth it. Even better, I hadn't hissed once. I think I deserve a few ticks on *my* chart.

Monday, 10 February

Still no letter. I can't take much more of this waiting. All the tension is pooling in my neck and across my shoulders. I woke at four this morning feeling as if someone had inserted a coat hanger across my shoulder blades. I gave up trying to sleep at six and came downstairs to try and coax them back into some degree of flexibility.

David came home from work this evening with some surprising news: an economy drive has been announced and forty jobs are going to be lost. We speculated about the possibility of his job being one of them. We'd be feeling very relieved now if we had that job offer in hand, but we don't. The timing of this announcement is bewildering. All along we've never doubted that David would have a job here if we didn't want to go north and now it seems that we may have needed this new job more than we'd ever imagined.

Only you know the future, Lord; help me to hang on in faith.

Tuesday, 11 February

Another early start and still no letter. Half-term starts at the end of this week and the children still don't know they are going to spend most of it in a cottage near Scardale.

Three different estate agents came today to value the house. We thought it would be helpful to know what our house might be worth before we look at houses next week. I spaced the appointments out so they didn't bump into each other, and by the last visit I would have made a good agent myself: 'back boiler, three double sockets, one radiator, double-glazing, yes, that's our garage, insulated loft, deceptively spacious . . .' and so on. In the end they came up with three different prices, with £12,000 difference between the lowest and the highest! I wondered why we'd bothered. We could have thought of a number and added some noughts all by ourselves.

It was a Readership training session in the evening, this time on prayer. I hadn't given it a lot of preparation and didn't really want to go, but at least it was a distraction. We were meant to (a) take along some personal item to talk about and (b) make some reflections on prayer. I hadn't twigged that (a) and (b) were meant to be connected, so I was very impressed when the first volunteer, a bird-watching enthusiast, brought out his binoculars and talked about how prayer brings God into focus. The next contribution was a reading from *Under Milk Wood* by a literature enthusiast. The connection with prayer wasn't quite so obvious, but at least he had style. Someone else brought a hand-painted bowl he'd been given by poverty-stricken Africans and talked about prayer being an offering of love. After this, my contribution to the evening was embarrassingly banal: I'd taken along a photo of the dog. I made something up about unquestioning devotion and got at least one encouraging smile from the only other pet lover in the group.

The best contribution came later during the general discussion on prayer. Pam breezily remarked that talking about prayer was a bit like talking about sex.

'It's a very personal activity and you can feel a failure when you listen to other people's experiences. There's even a temptation to exaggerate one's experiences so as not to feel a failure.' This observation had a remarkable effect on the group: all the women doubled over laughing in agreement and all the men solemnly inspected their shoes.

Readership training has its moments.

Thursday, 13 February

At last the long wait is over. The letter came yesterday. All the waiting and the recent anxiety about David's current job have combined to sweep away whatever remained of my resistance to the idea of moving. My overwhelming feeling is of sheer relief. David had felt all along that the job was right. I have been the churlish and ungrateful one who has fretted, worried and doubted my way through the last three months. I'm sorry, Lord.

We told the children after tea last night. It wasn't easy. At first Matthew cheered because he'd be nearer his friend's favourite football team, but then he saw his sister in tears. She cried for a full half-hour and insisted she wasn't going. In the end she did take a reluctant interest in the tourist brochures I'd kept from our day trip in January. Matthew's only question was, 'Do they speak English in Scardale?' Technically, the answer's yes.

By the time I tucked Emma into bed she had resolved to be brave. She picked up our church's Christmas card that had been by her bed and read out this year's motto verse: 'Be strong and courageous. Do not be terrified; do not be discouraged, for the LORD your God will be with you wherever you go' (Joshua 1:9). I told her that it was the first verse I'd ever memorised as a child and that it had meant so much to me over the years. I talked about my own memories of being wrenched away from friends and people I loved when I was her age, and there were a few more tears as we prayed together.

This morning I had a lump in my throat as I watched her go through the school gates. I don't know which has been harder to handle, her distress at the news last night or her determination to be brave this morning. I know she will tell her best friend today so I'd better call Best Friend's mum to forewarn her.

Friday, 14 February

Yesterday was mostly taken up with telling our

news to friends and neighbours. The neighbours bit was the worst: Frank and Mary next door have been so close to the kids. Ever since he could walk, Matthew has been climbing up for little chats with Frank over the garden fence.

I've felt very drained going over and over the same story with different people, but now that it's in the open I don't want anyone to be 'the last to find out'. My high spot in the day was Matthew coming out of school with a Valentine's Day card he'd just made for me. Inside he'd written, 'I love the world with all my heart'! That's Matthew for you. No obvious signs of distress there. Spent the evening packing for our 'holiday' in the north. We need to get an early start in the morning.

Thursday, 20 February

A half-term holiday in a little cottage on the edge of the moors – sounds idyllic, doesn't it? It wasn't. I am *so* relieved to be home.

The cottage wasn't only 'on the edge of the moor', it was also on the edge of civilisation. It was at the end of a mile-long farm track and the nearest shop was a ten-minute walk away. There was indeed an abundance of countryside, but rather too much weather to go with it. After the driest January for decades we went north during the wettest week of winter. The wind was gale force and the rain was incessant. The sun put in a half-hour appearance one morning to cries of 'My goodness, it *is* pretty round here' before the landscape was once again obscured by the banks of black clouds rolling in. It wasn't all torrential rain, mind you, we also had thunder and hailstorms just to add variety. Well, I was promised rain, after all . . .

It wouldn't have been so bad but we didn't even have the gear to cope with all this weather. David had made dire and unfounded predictions about the size of his mother's suitcase and we knew we needed the space for the three stuffed cake tins that would come with her. So we economised on the wet-weather gear: we had one rainproof anorak, one brolly and two child-sized wellies between five of us (not counting Gran's plastic rainhat).

The same lack of space in the car meant we had insufficient indoor entertainment suitable for rainy days on a freezing farm in February. The children only had a few books and felt pens and these provided about ten minutes of entertainment on the first morning. Just when we were getting desperate, Emma discovered an understairs cupboard. This yielded three ancient board games and, overjoyed, she settled on the least suitable and most complicated. Thankfully David was chosen to play it with them. The entire game took two days with short breaks for sleeping and eating. Poor David, it

'Walking an unobliging and terrified dog'

was a hard penance for forgetting to pack the Junior Scrabble.

My penance was the dog. As promised, there was no enclosed garden, only a farmyard complete with a tempting flock of chickens and ducks. Tempting to a dog, that is. This meant he couldn't go out unaccompanied and I was the adult who did all the accompanying, usually wearing two coats, borrowed wellies, a scarf and two pairs of gloves. Walking an unobliging and terrified dog at all hours of the day and night, in the teeth of a gale, on the edge of an inky black moor, was not my idea of fun. I'll sure I'll look back and laugh, eventually.

The one day we did plan some organised fun it nearly ended in disaster. I set off with Gran and the kids to find the local leisure facilities. 'Central Leisure' sounded like a plush, purpose-built, tropical-temperature, wave-machine wonderland. It wasn't. It was your typical red-brick Victorian baths. I got very lost and stressed trying to find it, and when we finally did fall through the doors and land at the wooden entry kiosk, an attendant dropped by to say the pool had just been closed. She nonchalantly informed us that the high winds had blown panes of glass from the ceiling into the swimming pool below! I didn't know whether to laugh or cry. Had we arrived on time we might have been sliced in two by falling glass; as it was we were only going to miss out on a swim. Divine intervention number one. In fact the cavernous building housed a smaller pool so we did actually get to swim, but I couldn't help keeping a nervous eye on the ceiling.

We were already tired and fed up before we got home that day. When we opened the door we found that the dog had eaten half the kitchen carpet. And when we opened the fridge door we found that the meat for our tea had gone off.

The dog didn't actually eat the carpet. He'd just discovered a loose thread that, when pulled, unravelled lots of lovely stringy stuff. In less than two hours he'd shredded a third of the floor area. I can't really blame him: we had left him in a freezing cold and unfamiliar kitchen, the wind howling round the house had terrified him and he had no idea that we wouldn't be long, so he had to make some protest. Considering the mess, the landlady was pretty reasonable about it.

The fact that the kitchen was so cold was actually a blessing in disguise, as the reason the meat went off was because neither of us had remembered to turn the fridge on. Our excuse is that we rarely turn our own fridge either on or off, so it didn't occur to either of us to check the status of the fridge in the cottage (mutual recriminations are still rumbling on). I only found out that the fridge had been off for the whole five days half an hour before we were due to leave. I was idling by the kettle and flicked a switch: the fridge came on.

I felt sick within seconds. No wonder the meat had gone off and Emma had had an upset tummy. We'd been eating food from an unchilled fridge for five days. I made David promise not to tell his mother! ('What the eye doesn't see . . .') The fact that nothing else had gone off, nor had anyone else been ill, was mostly due to the chill of the kitchen. Divine intervention number two.

The good news is: we got home in one piece. The not-so-good news is that we are going back there . . . permanently (thankfully, not to that precise location). So much for it being an upbeat, positive experience for the children. Oh well, I guess it can only get better.

I think I'll have to rely on a few more interventions of the divine variety.

Friday, 21 February

My sister called this evening and heard the whole story of our week away. I was bemoaning the abundance of rain and the lack of clear direction. We had gone up there, praying hard, with our ears pinned back (spiritually speaking) and the whole week was a wash-out in every way. I hated Scardale, none of the schools we visited could offer us places and the only house we liked turned out to be in a red-light district. I even confessed my failure to find a green door. (The intensity of my desire to find a new nest for my brood had given me embarrassing spiritual delusions the week before we went away. After one particularly intense prayer session I felt I was being given the sign of 'green door'. I must have been screwing my eyes up too tight, I never saw a green door all week.) My sister consoled me with wise words about God giving us a mind and the common sense to work out for ourselves where we should live, and later sent me the words of a worship song she'd been listening to all week: 'Sometimes He Comes in the Rain'!

Sunday, 23 February

It's been a weekend for seeing old friends. Yesterday we returned to the place where we used to live before we lived here, for a wedding reception. Many good friends from our previous church were there, some of whom we hadn't seen for the whole five years since our last move.

Going in was a bit scary. I recognised people who greeted me warmly while I was mentally scrambling to remember their names. In fact, forgetting names didn't matter. These were minor details compared to the warm feeling of being back again with people with whom we'd shared a critical period of our lives. I got quite nostalgic.

My ego also received a huge boost when someone asked us how we could go away for five years and come back looking five years younger. (This particular optical illusion is achieved by the purchase of contact lenses for me and the removal of a moustache for David.) Everyone asked how old the children were and expressed astonishment that Emma was now eight and Matthew six. Why is it that when children move away from us and out of sight we expect them to stand still? I was equally astonished to hear about the children who used to be in our old Pathfinder group, who were now in their final year at university. In my mind's eye I can only recall them as awkward thirteen-year-olds. How can they possibly be driving cars, taking degrees and marrying people?

Someone has pressed the fast forward button on time. I'm not sure when it happened; perhaps it was when Matthew started school, a day I thought would never come during that long period of full-time motherhood. Time may move us inexorably onwards but my distinct impression is that it's moving me on faster than it used to.

Today we caught up with another set of old friends over lunch and celebrated their daughter's eleventh birthday. How can a child be eleven when I remember her arrival as if it were yesterday? I'm beginning to understand what people mean by a mid-life crisis, but I don't feel old enough to have one. Sometimes I still think about what I'd like to be when I grow up!

By June of this year I will reach the mid-life point (assuming the biblical average of three score and ten). This will coincide with our move north. I'm hoping it will be an opportunity for the ref to blow the whistle for half-time and let me retreat to the dressing-room to catch my breath and take stock of the game so far.

It's dawning on me more and more that life is a team game, and my own abilities will only get me so far. Without a good team, my family, and a set of faithful supporters cheering from the sidelines, my friends, I'd probably have fallen flat on my face a long time ago. I'm finding it hard to know I have to leave yet another set of friends behind and start over again. The only thing that keeps me going is the fact that God has hand-picked me for his team and has dressed me in his colours. This gives me hope for the second half.

Monday, 24 February

Tonight I met my 'team' from church. Together we run the Sunday school. This was our first meeting after I'd told them individually that I wouldn't be able to carry on after Easter – not great news for a team that struggles for members at the best of times. Their understanding and support was very moving. We prayed hard for new leaders. There's an open meeting for anyone interested on Thursday.

Thursday, 27 February

I spent all morning preparing for this evening's open meeting for prospective Sunday school teachers. No one came. Actually that's not quite true, one of the current team members turned up to keep me company. I appreciated his support. As to the lack of new volunteers, disappointed isn't the word for it. Sometimes serving sucks.

Friday, 28 February

The house was in the paper for the first time last night; we'll see if we get any response this weekend. David has one month left of churchwarden duties. Tonight his duty is to go out and listen to the grievances of residents who have to live next to our church hall. This will be an exercise in tact and diplomacy, during which he hopes to pour large quantities of oil on very troubled waters. I hope he's successful. At least someone will definitely come to his meeting; people who want to complain usually have no trouble turning up to meetings.

It's probably fair to say that we have both been wearied by our church responsibilities. David will finish at the end of March and I will give up Sunday school at the end of April, at which point I hope we'll find some free weekends to go house-hunting.

Saturday, 1 March

Woke up far too early this morning with a pain in the neck and 'to do' list on my mind. I suspect the two were connected. I gave up on sleep and came downstairs to enjoy some peace and quiet before the kids got up. The dog was pleased to see me. I made a cup of tea and thought about everything I had to do. My head swam. My Readership tutor has persuaded me to complete the Preaching module on the Readership course before I leave; this means that in the next five weeks I must write four sermon outlines and one whole sermon. In real life, there is also another sermon to prepare for Mother's Day in a week's time. On top of this I also have a whole term's Sunday school curriculum to sort out, several new leaders to find from goodness knows where, a house to sell, children to nurture, a husband to love and a dog to walk (those last three items qualify as pleasures, not chores, but it's still a job to find time for them).

When I look beyond all this frenetic activity and actually think about what it will be like to arrive 'up north' and have no commitments, I feel terror and relief in equal proportions. Relief because I feel I'm more than ready for some time on the sidelines, and terror because it feels that life as we know it will come to an end. It's as if I'm attached to an electronic heart monitor: my pulse may be frantic, my blood pressure high, but at least I'm alive, the wiggly green line across the screen is evidence of that. I'm worried that by the time I get to June the line will go straight. I'm probably being melodramatic.

Came across a line from a poem in my Bible notes,

> Turn the weak moonlight of my faith
> To brighter faith,
> In which I see your radiance,
> Know your love.

Prayer seemed the only appropriate response.

Sunday, 2 March

No viewings all weekend. Perhaps it was a little unrealistic to expect prospective purchasers to be queuing down the drive? Plucked up the courage to make one more call to a contact 'up north'. I rang a minister in a town near where we hope to live. It proved a very fruitful conversation. His description of his own church gave me misgivings, but his description of another church in the area intrigued me. He mentioned a church in a village 'over the hill': Shawcross. I'd never heard of Shawcross before and it took me quite a while to find it on the map. Cross-referencing several other information booklets revealed that Shawcross had not only a church, but also a school and a post office. This was beginning to sound like a possibility. It's long been a prayer-dream of mine to live, work, worship and send the children to school, all in the same community. Perhaps this was it?

Monday, 3 March

The problem with Mondays is that they are too short. This morning I had an article to write and an agenda to prepare, there were piles of washing shouting at me from the kitchen and at least four phone calls to be made. So why did I give in to the compulsive desire to tidy Matthew's bedroom? Now I'm even further behind and could do with a few more hours in the day.

The trouble with working from home is that you have to learn to ignore the housework, and some days I simply can't. I do not cope well with an untidy environment so the route to my desk is strewn with obstacles such as Hoovers, floor mops and piles of washing.

It was Plough Monday a few Mondays ago. Matthew told me so and his teacher had told him, so it must be true. I'd never heard of Plough Monday. Was it a seasonal warm-up for Shrove Tuesday? A hang-over from our agricultural past? I'm not sure what one is meant to do on a Plough Monday (apart from the obvious) but this morning it struck me as a very good description of Mondays in general and today in particular: too many tasks and too little time. I want to do everything and I want to do it all now.

I did at least make time to read. I'm reading Numbers at the moment; this morning I reached chapter 11 and spent a happy few moments finding fault with my fellow Christians. Moses is really fed up. He's had to lead a group of moaning miseries through the desert and he's had enough. I know just how he feels. Some people just don't seem to want to get to the promised land. I've heard no end of moans in our church lately: 'Why are we doing this? Where are we going next? Who's going to lead us? Where on earth will the money come from?' It really must get the clergy down.

Then I got to verse 23: 'Is the LORD's arm too short?' and found myself convicted of my own private moaning and the disbelief it represents: 'Where are we going? When are we going to get there? And how will we ever afford it?' I have to admit I've been guilty of dragging my metaphorical feet over our own private journey to our particular 'promised land'.

Thinking about the Lord's arm being too short reminds me of my dad. He was very tall and very big and when I was little I really believed he was a giant. On Sundays, when we often had visitors, he used to sit at one end of our long dining-table and yet he could reach over and pass you anything you wanted from the other end of the table. As a small child I was so in awe of this ability I actually believed his arms were extendable; that they could stretch and retract like a Stretch Armstrong toy. I've never quite recovered from this childish confidence in a huge, all-powerful father. Just as well, really.

Wednesday, 5 March

Still reading Numbers, reached chapter 15: 'When you enter the land I am giving you as a home . . . do not forget the LORD.' Seems like good advice to me.

Friday, 7 March

Spent the whole day writing the family service talk. Mother's Day has arrived, somewhat inconveniently, halfway through our series of family services on Old Testament stories. We have been trying to be chronologically correct, hence Noah in January and Joseph in February. In April we do Joshua, so for this month we needed a mother somewhere between the Patriarchs and the promised land. We landed on Jochebed, the mother of Moses, arguably the most obscure mother in the whole Bible! But on Mother's Day there is no such thing as an obscure mother, 'the hand that rocks the cradle rules the world' and all that. Jochebed didn't actually rock her son's cradle, mind you, she covered it in tar and launched it on the Nile, but I'm sure it was an act of faith. I hope so, anyway; that's what my sermon's about. The other two hazards in the service are a game involving a jigsaw in which one piece is required to be missing, and a distribution of flowers which requires three daffodils for every female in church.

Sunday, 9 March

Mother's Day: I didn't get breakfast in bed but I didn't complain. We had to be up early and ready for church because we were leaving straight after for David's sister's to have lunch with Gran. At least I didn't have to cook today.

The family service went well. The game worked, there were enough flowers for everyone and my story about Three Women and a Baby seemed to go down okay.

David's sister Becky has two cats so we didn't think it would be a good idea to take Chester (entertaining, possibly, but not a good idea). Jane and David kindly agreed to have him for the day. We picked him up on our way home only to find he'd thrown up on their carpet and then escaped into the neighbour's garden. Will this dog never learn to impress anyone?

No viewers again this weekend. Perhaps we've pitched the price too high.

Wednesday, 12 March

The children are coping reasonably well with the prospect of moving north, which is a big answer to prayer. Emma has been rather over-excited and boisterous all week but her parents' state of distraction probably hasn't helped. David is very busy trying to tie up all the loose ends of his old job and I am only a quarter of the way through my 'to do' list from ten days ago.

We are getting plenty of post from the north. If it's not a school prospectus, it's a list of properties for sale. Emma loves opening these and is now considering a career as an estate agent. She scrutinises every line of every house description, which has raised some interesting questions. So far we have explained: 'cornice', 'dog-leg', 'GFCH' and 'mezzanine' (although we weren't too sure about that last one). Her preference would be a three-storey, six-bedroom Victorian affair complete with cellars but I keep telling her not to get her hopes up, we still haven't sold.

I'm pleased she is looking ahead positively; my problem is not to look ahead too far. Sometimes my sights are fixed so far ahead of myself, it's a job to focus on today. But today is the only gift I have and to live it faithfully is the challenge. It would be a shame to wish away the present as we stretch towards the future.

Saturday, 15 March

I met with all the Sunday school leaders last night. It was a hundred per cent improvement on the open meeting when nobody turned up. The summer programme seems to be falling into place and the enthusiasm of the few faithful leaders did much to lift my spirits.

There are no viewers lined up for this weekend, again. We began discussing our options. We will either have to reduce our price or be prepared to wait. I hate waiting. David hates reducing the price.

I've finished reading Numbers; this morning I started Deuteronomy. I had to smile at verse 6 of chapter 1: 'You have stayed long enough' . . . you've doubted, you've grumbled, you've sent out your spies and now it's time to move on, so 'do not be terrified; do not be afraid' (verse 29). Forgive me if I'm taking this all too personally, Lord, but it all sounds so relevant. I'm ready to go. There's just one small problem: a buyer would be nice.

Sunday, 16 March

Matthew brought Sunday lunch to a standstill today.

'Mum,' he asked casually, 'you know the forty days and forty nights when Jesus was in Kent . . .'

Forks stopped in mid-air, we looked at each other

blankly and a line from 'Jerusalem' went through my head. Well, 'did those feet, in ancient times, walk upon England's mountains green?' According to Matthew it seems they did.

My next thought was to offer my resignation as a Sunday school leader on the grounds of unbiblical teaching but before I got round to a response, Emma interjected.

'In *Kent*, Matthew? Grandma lives in Kent.'

Sensing that something was not quite right, he changed tack.

'We're in it now . . . you're meant to give up sweets.'

'Lent! You mean Lent!' we all chorused simultaneously. Poor lad, we never did find out what he wanted to say about it.

Monday, 17 March

This was the Monday Matthew ran out of grey trousers. It wasn't an oversight on the domestic front, there were plenty of clean pairs in his wardrobe, but suddenly none of them seemed to fit. He must have had the fastest growth spurt on record. On Friday there hadn't been anything wrong with his school trousers, this morning there were two inches of fresh air around his ankles.

We had long blue trousers, of course, and green ones, but no long grey ones and only grey would do.

'The fastest growth spurt on record'

Thankfully we had grey shorts, which seemed acceptable. On the way to school I was self-consciously explaining the choice of shorts to a friend who comforted me immensely by telling me that she'd just heard a severe weather warning on the radio. Matthew looked alarmed. Would it be snow? Torrential rain? Hail? No, none of the above. Today's hazard was fog. I pointed out to him that a pair of bright white knees could be a positive asset given the conditions. He was not amused.

Friday, 21 March

All week I've dreaded the disappointment of no one coming to see the house this weekend and today (oh, joy) two people have made appointments. I threw myself into a cleaning frenzy and momentarily contemplated tidying the children into a cupboard. Perhaps I ought to arrange to take them out.

Saturday, 22 March

I am thinking of becoming a nun.

I think I received a calling to the contemplative life today in Tesco's. I'd only gone in for two packets of dog food and ten minutes' peace, but solitude and silence can do wonderful things for you, even in the dog-food aisle of a supermarket.

I'm not being serious about the nun bit. I realise

I've already blown my chances. As a married mother of two, obedience and poverty are second nature, but celibacy would be tricky. For the most part I'm content with my lot; delusions of sisterhood only come over me every time I have to spend a Saturday shopping with the children.

Today we had to go shoe-shopping. This is the worst kind of shopping with children. Buying them shoes is a fraught and expensive business, all the more so now that they have opinions about shoes, opinions that are usually bigger than our budget. They also loathe shopping. Given this toxic mixture of attitudes, David came along for moral support.

First we shoe-horned Matthew into a suitable pair of trainers in Woolworth's. He wasn't keen.

'They feel uncomfortable after a while,' he explained, having had them on his feet for ten seconds. Objection over-ruled, item one purchased.

Next I found a pair in the sale for Emma. The fact that they were reduced made it virtually certain that she wouldn't like them. She didn't.

They fitted a treat.

'I won't wear them,' she threatened. As the only other footwear she owns is a pair of wellies, I felt I was on safe ground. Item number two in the bag.

We only remembered the dog food on the way home in the car. I don't know why it occurred to us at that point: perhaps the prodding, whining and howling from the back seat had something to do with it, but that was just the kids (why is it that having to share the back seat of a car with your brother constitutes a major invasion of personal space?).

Nobly I offered to drop everyone off at home and go back for the dog food on my own. All I really wanted was the ten minutes' silence each way. It was bliss, hence the nun fantasy.

We haven't heard back from today's viewers. The kids at least behaved themselves, which is more than can be said for the dog. Perhaps we should have tied him up at the end of the garden.

Wednesday, 26 March

Back in Tesco's again. My last chance to shop in peace before school holidays. They break up today and we go off to Spring Harvest tomorrow. We are looking forward to this annual extravaganza of teaching, worship, fellowship and sleeplessness. It's not exactly a rest but it's usually refreshing.

I wonder if they do silent 'try it for size' sessions for would-be nuns? I doubt it somehow, but the idea appeals.

Monday, 31 March – Easter Monday

It was warm enough to sit on the beach today, even to paddle in the sea. 'Skegness in the Springtime', what a pleasant surprise. It's been good to get away. The children have enjoyed their groups, had a go at abseiling and been swimming every day. We have enjoyed time with friends and time with God.

Time together will be at a premium for the next few months. David starts his new job this week and will be away almost all week every week until we can get up north to join him. Our hope is to get the children into their new school for the second half of this summer term so that they will have time to make friends before the long summer break, but as half-term is only eight weeks away and we haven't even got a buyer yet, this looks unlikely. We'll just have to trust God's timing.

Tuesday, 1 April

April Fool's Day and David's first day with his new employer. Just as well we're not superstitious. He had to take his first day as holiday anyway because we were coming home from Spring Harvest today. Pleased to discover that the agent had shown two people round the house while we'd been away but no offers as yet.

Wednesday, 2 April

Got up at 6.30 a.m. to wave David off. Such wifely devotion won't last but I thought I'd better make an effort on his first day. He is being put up in a hotel for the first six weeks he's away. This week he'll be back on Friday and next week he'll only be away for Monday and Tuesday, so he's suggested I go up with him on Sunday and have a look round the area while he's at work. The children are still off school so someone would be needed to hold the fort at home. Will ring Grandma today and ask if she can come up and help us out.

Thursday, 3 April

I'm all on my own tonight. When you live 'cheek by jowl' in a small house with three other people, it feels very odd to suddenly find yourself alone. The luxury is that I do not have to jostle for time in the bathroom, nor do I have to tolerate anyone else's choice of music or television programme. The reality is that I can't think of any music I want to listen to and I've started to talk to the dog.

Thankfully this solitary situation is temporary. David returns tomorrow and the children are only on overnight sleep-overs with friends. Emma has only been for a sleep-over once before; tonight she is staying with her best friend and has opted to go without 'Fleecy' (her night-time 'cuddly') so she must be growing up.

Matthew complained loudly that he'd never been on a sleep-over, so he was delighted when I told him some friends had invited him to stay. He raced off straight away to pack a suitcase. Unfortunately he doesn't own a suitcase, but he made up for this fact by stuffing his wash bag with all the essentials: four cuddly toys and a pair of pyjamas!

Personally I think there is 'no place like home' but I'm also quite pleased that neither of them are fazed by the idea of waking up in someone else's house and eating someone else's breakfast cereal. By the time we finally complete the process of moving up north they may well have to spend several more nights with close friends.

I have secretly enjoyed being a recluse for twenty-four hours. I was even tempted to take the phone off the hook but I worried about Matthew missing me. He didn't. And, thankfully, no one else rang. It's not that I've gone off my friends, it's just that all my conversations seem rather repetitive these days: 'Any news about your house yet?', 'When do you hope to move?', 'Do you know where you'll be living?' All well-meant enquiries which wouldn't be half so irritating if only I knew the answers. Perhaps I should wear a badge: 'Don't Ask!' Then again, perhaps not.

If I'm feeling weary of this process, how much more weary must God be with my constant petitions. I feel like a small child on the back seat of a car, half an hour into a long journey, saying 'Are we nearly there yet?' every five minutes. I've no idea where 'there' is nor do I know the length of the journey. What's more I have a sneaky anxiety that when we finally arrive I will put my head out the window and yell, 'Where on earth are we?' but for the time being at least I just have to keep reminding myself who is in the driving seat.

Friday, 4 April

Slept dreadfully, woke with every creak and bump all night long. Couldn't bear to look in on the empty, unusually tidy bedrooms this morning. Busied myself with cleaning the house all morning in the hope that some more viewings would be booked this weekend (at least that's what I told myself; my mother's imminent arrival is purely coincidental). I was rewarded at lunchtime when the estate agent phoned with a viewing in the afternoon. Fortunately I could leave the agent to it. The kids came home after lunch and, before they could leave their usual untidy impression, I whisked them down the street to visit a friend. We even took the dog with us this time.

I am trying not to hope too much. It would be amazingly convenient to have a buyer hooked the day before we set off for three days' house-hunting in the north but, as David always says, 'counting chickens is an exercise for foolish optimists'; perhaps that's why it comes naturally to me.

David arrived home very late having battled

through the Friday night traffic. It took him four hours to do a journey that should have taken two but it was 'only to be expected' (serious pessimists like him are rarely disappointed).

Grandma arrives tomorrow to allow David and me to go back up north on Sunday to house-hunt together.

Saturday, 5 April

We've sold! We've sold! Joy and jubilation. For once my optimism has paid off, but even I can hardly believe it and David certainly can't. Five weeks on the market and we've sold to a first-time buyer no less, so no chain. By our standards of selling houses this is astonishingly good news. David had seriously expected at least a six-month wait to sell (and with faith like that it's a wonder we have sold!). Suddenly our hopes for moving in the June half-term are back on the agenda.

In all my excitement, however, I hadn't antici-pated the children's reaction. When I announced to them that we'd sold the house they both burst into tears. This wasn't the reaction I expected. Having had the 'For Sale' board outside for five weeks I'd assumed they'd realised its purpose. Of course, they did know we were moving, but selling seemed so final somehow that, in spite of their previous bravery, they took it hard. Matthew in particular has no idea of the time-scale involved, so when David prayed with him tonight at bedtime he wondered if we were moving out tomorrow. It took more than a few minutes to try and explain all the if's, but's and maybe's involved in selling a house and it wasn't easy. I so hope this sale goes through – I couldn't face the kids being messed about.

Tuesday, 8 April

Grandma and the kids, all still in their pyjamas, waved us off at eight o'clock on Sunday morning. By half ten we were parking up outside the little church in Shawcross, and I took a deep breath before going in. It was hard to keep an open mind when I had such a feeling of 'this is the place'. Peter, who we'd spoken to on the phone, met us at the door and guided us to a pew.

On the way up in the car we had discussed what we hoped to achieve. Expecting to find a house, a school and a church all in three days would be pushing it. David suggested we concentrate on narrowing the area. We could live anywhere within a twenty-mile radius of his work, which gave us an awful lot of houses, churches and schools to choose from, so the whole decision would be easier if we could at least settle on a location.

Apart from church in the morning Sunday wasn't

a very successful day. We pottered around some villages, had lunch in a pub and tried, unsuccessfully, to go to an evening service at a different church. Peter and his wife had kindly invited us back for some supper later that evening, and they lifted our spirits by giving us a long list of ideas and possibilities as well as praying with us.

I faced Monday with fresh courage and a firm grip on the A-to-Z. After dropping David at work I had eight hours on my own to explore. I did two towns and several more villages, which was going some. Then we saw two houses in the evening. This morning I explored yet another town but nothing had appealed to me as much as the village of Shawcross. I drove back through it on my way home this afternoon, stopping to buy some flowers for Mum and lingering hopefully in the main street. I don't know what I was hoping for; a neon sign in the sky with the words 'This is it' and a large arrow might have been nice, but guidance is never that straightforward. Pity, really.

Wednesday, 9 April

The last day of the school holidays. Mum went home this morning. She and the kids had had a great time without us: walking the dog, going on picnics, and eating at McDonald's (how to impress one's grandchildren in three easy steps). The children quickly realised that Grandma turns a better blind eye than Mummy and made the most of this fact in the garden: Emma had built a tree house in a laurel bush and Matthew had dug a huge pit under a conifer.

'The pit is for the time capsule,' they explained.

Silly me, I should have guessed. Today they busied themselves putting it together: a few not-too-precious toys, a letter and a map were ceremoniously shoved into a bottle and buried in the pit. The dog, who had enjoyed the digging bit, looked very depressed to see it filled in. The children seem pleased to have left some evidence of their existence, but I'm not sure what the buyer will make of the burial mound in her garden.

Sunday, 13 April

Family service again, Joshua this time. And my debut as a rap artiste! A talented member of our congregation had written a mini musical, no less, which told the whole story of Joshua in songs and raps. The performance was meant to culminate with the collapse of the walls of Jericho.

This isn't the first time we have attempted to re-enact an act of God. We parted the Red Sea last year, but it wasn't convincing. We were hoping for a bigger effect this time but it has called for some subtle engineering. David, my conveniently scientific,

'The pit is for the time capsule'

churchwarden husband, has been assigned to supervise the surreptitious demolition of our cardboard-box wall. The tricky bit was making it fall on cue.

In rehearsal yesterday he spent ages fiddling with string and sticky tape and promised us that the wall would fall, as required, at the end of the final number. When we reached the last note and stamped our feet the wall was meant to topple dramatically and crash to the ground. Instead we stamped our feet, David pulled his string and one box slid sideways, leaving all the rest stubbornly in place and all the performers in fits of laughter.

'Not enough string', apparently. This morning, armed with several rolls of the stuff, he promised me the wall *would* fall on cue, but we didn't have time for a rehearsal. The children sang and rapped their way through the programme and at the final moment, bang on cue, the wall teetered, tumbled and finally crashed to cheers of victory and surprise from a latter-day bunch of faithless Israelites.

David tried not to look as relieved as he felt.

To finish we taught the final part of our four-part memory verse: 'And he will make your paths straight' (Proverbs 3:5,6). It's been astonishing how relevant these verses have been to our own personal journey. I feel I have lived each service as I have prepared it.

Wednesday, 16 April

On Monday I started out the week, strong in the confidence that the Lord 'will make your paths straight' but already it's been a week of great highs and lows. First I rang the school in Shawcross to enquire about places. Yes, they had places for both children. As this was only the second school to offer us places out of the twenty I've so far tried I was somewhat surprised, and instead of being pleased I immediately worried: why did they have spaces? weren't they a good school? (there's no pleasing some people). Then I explained to the school secretary that we didn't live in the area just yet but we were hoping to find a house soon. 'You don't happen to know any for sale, do you?' I added for good measure.

'Well, it's funny you should say that . . .' she replied and I felt the hairs rise on the back of my neck. 'My neighbour is about to put her house on the market . . . shall I get her to call you?' I stammered out a surprised 'yes' and left my number.

We were both excited when the call came on Monday evening. The house was in just the right location, it was almost the same size as ours, it had the right size garden, it had potential to extend, it even had a garage. David was looking over my shoulder as I jotted it all down, muttering 'yes, yes, yes'. And then I asked the price.

Oh no, what a blow! A mere £25,000 more than

we can afford. Disappointment has hung over us like a cloud ever since. I made the mistake of telling someone all about it on the phone last night and all they gave me in return was someone else's house-selling horror story. This response was straight from the 'there's-someone-worse-off-than-you' school of comfort and it didn't help at all; now I am not only disappointed, I also feel guilty about feeling disappointed. I also feel frustrated. If I did a 'proper job' instead of all this part-time stuff designed to fit around the kids we'd be able to afford that house. But being ambitious for a bigger income seems very materialistic and self-centred, which doesn't help my prayers. Yet another Job's comforter spent a long time trying to distract me by telling me all about a missionary she knew who'd given up everything to go and live and work among prostitutes in King's Cross. Such selfless devotion only made me feel even more inadequate: who am I, a mere middle-class mother, home-maker, part-time 'this and that person' to expect Almighty God to be interested in our perceived lack of funds?

I've felt miserable, uncomfortable and under-mined all week. The dream of living in Shawcross seems to be slipping away.

Friday, 18 April

Yet more bad news. We decided in the week that

if we couldn't find somewhere we could afford to buy in Shawcross then we'd rent somewhere in Shawcross and wait for a suitable house. However, this morning the bank told us that if we closed down our mortgage they'd charge us a huge penalty because we are only halfway through a three-year deal we tied ourselves into when we extended last year. This clarifies our options. Plan A: sell this house and buy another, no penalty to pay; or Plan B: sell this house and rent, pay a huge penalty.

Saturday, 19 April

Woke up with two monsters, one on each shoulder. They introduced themselves as Self-pity and Worry. I told them to get lost but they didn't seem to notice. Still feeling condemned because I haven't been called to a sacrificial ministry among prostitutes in King's Cross. Why on earth did I think God would be interested in *my* problems?

I held hands with the monsters until David got up and restored my perspective.

'It's simple,' he said, 'we've found the location, the church is right, the school is right, we just have to hold on in faith for the right house.'

'Simple,' he says. Okay, I can do simple. The monsters sloped quietly away from the sunshine of his faith.

Sunday, 20 April

No monsters this morning, and the opportunity for a lie-in followed by a leisurely breakfast for two because both kids spent last night with friends. We had turned in late, safe in the knowledge we could sleep in as long as we liked.

But it was not to be. The doorbell rang at 8.00 a.m. It didn't just ring once. It rang continuously for the whole time it took me to wake up, groan, roll over, look at the clock, groan again, stagger out of bed, find my dressing-gown, stumble down the stairs, find the door keys and open the door.

'You have a big problem,' my neighbour told me. ('So have you, mate,' I almost replied.) 'Your drains are blocked and if you flush the loo one more time the inspection pit will overflow into your garden.'

This was not music to my ears, but I did at least thank my informant. The fact that I had been sound asleep and hadn't even been thinking of flushing my loo seemed irrelevant. Now that he'd mentioned it, I wanted to flush it very badly!

David got up and did his best Victor Meldrew impression all the way to the phone. Fortunately we have several friends who own rods for clearing drains. We woke two of them before we found some rods to borrow. David then spent the next hour 'down the pit'.

Keeping well out of the way, I managed to wash at the garden tap and headed off for church where I was due to meet the kids. By the time David arrived everyone had heard the story and he was greeted with loud remarks about his 'blockage' and offered a pew of his own!

After the service someone I didn't know very well came up to me and told me that she'd been praying for us all week, now that our house had sold, knowing we couldn't find anywhere to live (but not knowing how I'd been feeling all week). The Lord had told her that we would 'live under the shadow of the Almighty' and she so exuded confidence and faith that it brought a lump to my throat. What a wonderful thought, living under God's protection and cover; it sounds a good place to be, I could go for that. There's just one thing, Lord, could you supply an address for that location? Even a map reference would be nice.

Okay, okay, I guess I'll just have to trust.

Monday, 21 April

David left at six this morning to work all week up north. He went armed with an A-to-Z, an Ordnance Survey map and several sets of house details. The poor lad has to work by day and house-hunt by night. We really need to find somewhere to live soon or our buyer might get impatient.

Typically for a Monday, David could leave as

early and as loudly as he liked and neither of the children stirred. On Saturday, when I woke at six with the monsters and longed to read in peace downstairs, I knew that as soon as I put one foot on the landing both children would bounce out of bed and expect the day to begin.

Eventually I heaved the kids out of bed at eight and got them to school on time. For a week now I have been trying to make time to read them a Bible story over breakfast. I knew this was over-ambitious. This morning there was no time and no Bible. The dog ate it yesterday.

It was probably my fault for leaving a temptingly large portion of the Word of God on the dining-room table where I thought it was out of reach. Giving the dog his tea on time would also have helped. As it was, we went out for two hours and returned to find a heavy hard-backed Children's Bible in shreds on the floor and the dog looking sheepish under the sofa. I'm having misgivings about this dog. His pedigree came in the post the other week and apparently his grandfather was called 'Original Sin'. Perhaps his breeding is getting the better of him.

Thursday, 24 April

David has rung home every night with the latest house details. I'm giving myself a headache trying to imagine houses I haven't seen and driving David barmy by asking questions about things he doesn't remember. He has settled on three houses to take us back to on Saturday when we are all going up for the day.

My stomach is churning with anxiety and my whole body feels tense with the need to make a decision.

Saturday, 26 April

I was awake from five o'clock anticipating the day ahead. I can't seem to sleep for more than five hours at a stretch. I wake with the birds and start wandering around the A-to-Z in my head and plan extensions on houses I haven't even seen. David saw seven houses this week, out of which he chose the ones we saw today.

David and I have such different approaches to house-buying, it's a wonder we ever agree. I rely on intuition and he relies on facts and figures. I ask, 'Does it have character?' and he asks, 'Is there room for the washing machine?' I wonder if it will make a happy home and he wonders if the window frames need painting. I've learnt that both viewpoints are invaluable, but also that two such different approaches can easily turn a discussion into an argument. The fact that we were allowing the children to take part in the debate could have stretched our arbitration skills to the limit.

But we did it! We all agreed on the same house. We looked at four in the end: (1) tall and thin with no garden or garage; (2) long and narrow with some garden and no garage; (3) plain and practical with everything at a price; and (4) tatty but different with a roofless garage and a wilderness for a garden. We went for number 4. The kids liked the garden because it was wild and hilly. David liked the kitchen because it was plumbed for everything, and I liked . . . well, it took me a while to decide what I liked.

Intuition was useless, there were no 'signs' or vibes to pick up; a strong imagination was what was required. It would need redecorating throughout, the drive re-laying and the front door re-positioning. When I stood and screwed my eyes up fairly tightly I could just about imagine what it could become.

And it isn't in the village. It's over the hill, about ten minutes away by car. David has adjusted his 'holding out in faith for the right house' line in the light of the bank's insistence that we have another mortgage. This is rather disappointing, but so long as I'm prepared to drive them there, the children can still go to the school in the village. We are looking at the house as a short-term stepping-stone. Move once and move again in a year or two. It doesn't sound an exciting route to take but it seems to be the only one available at the moment. A line from a recent sermon has stuck in my mind: 'Seventy years from now we'll all be in Heaven anyway.' Seen from that perspective, our earthly location does seem rather unimportant. I hope we've made the right choice. Our offer was accepted.

Sunday, 27 April

My last morning in Sunday school. I was presented with a surprise bunch of flowers and some lovely gifts, some of them made by the children. Felt a bit tearful.

Tuesday, 29 April

My last session of Readership training. Another presentation of a farewell gift. Very touched by people's kindness. Couldn't find the words to say goodbye.

Wednesday, 30 April

Finished my final writing project before we move. Sent it off, feeling fairly numb. Having to move through all these 'endings' on auto-pilot. As for faith, I'm leaning hard on David's. Mine feels like a piece of elastic that's spent the last few months being stretched and stretched. I've been pulled by so many commitments and decisions that now they are all over and the decision's been made, it feels like the elastic's just snapped – ping! – and I feel no good to anyone. Still, at least all that is required of me in the coming month is to go through the house, room by room, and sort, condense and pack all our belongings. That, and face a continual round of goodbyes.

Saturday, 3 May

We've come down to Somerset this weekend to see some old friends. It's not really a 'goodbye' visit because these are friends with whom we've stayed in touch through several moves. We are aware, though, that once we go north, Somerset will seem like a long way for a weekend jaunt. The weather has been kind and the children have played out in the garden all afternoon, mostly constructing dens. It's been good to get away and have the time to talk things over with familiar friends.

Monday, 5 May

Today I start upstairs. My task is to go through the place room by room, minimising our belongings. I'm not a hoarder by nature so I find it quite cathartic to clear out clothes that no longer fit, toys that no longer work and gadgets we no longer need. The only things I hoard are books. I can't bring myself to part with a book, even if I have read it till the pages are falling out (or perhaps especially if I've read it that much).

Saturday, 10 May

The children were in experimental mode today. Emma wrote another experimental cake recipe and Matthew spent the morning attempting to create curds and whey by vigorously shaking half a cup of skimmed milk with a pat of butter in a Tupperware beaker. I don't know what has inspired either of them – something on morning television perhaps; on Saturdays they are allowed to slip down and watch it while we slumber on.

Emma delivered her 'recipe' to me just as I struggled towards consciousness this morning. Contemplating the combination of cinnamon, baking powder and chocolate was not the ideal way to wake up. As this is not her first experimental cake, I've learnt that turning a blind eye is the best policy. She is an independent cook who seems to think that following pre-prepared recipes is only for wimps. She likes to stride out into the unknown, to boldly go where no cook has gone before. If the end result is edible it's a bonus.

By mid-morning Matthew's one-man dairy factory was running out of steam as he realised that shaking the beaker for the required minimum of three hours might be somewhat tiring. He offered to share the chore around.

But David and I had enough chores of our own. No hitches so far with the sale of this house, and steady progress on our purchase of the 'dump', as we have come to call it. As 'the dump' is currently unoccupied there is no reason why we shouldn't move sooner rather than later. David would prefer sooner. Today he started working on the extremities of our belongings: clearing the shed, the garage and the loft.

I would prefer later. I kept myself busy today with any task that had nothing to do with moving because, in spite of the fact that I've spent the whole week packing, there is a part of me that is refusing to believe that we are actually moving. I don't know if reality will hit me before the removal van rolls up at the door. If it doesn't I'm in for a shock.

The thought of living in a street where I don't know a soul rather unnerves me. Nor have we finally decided where we will send the children to school. I don't know where to shop, where to post letters or where to walk the dog. Abraham may have followed God to an unknown destination but I need an address, a tourist information booklet and a list of schools.

I like the familiar recipes for life. Perhaps I ought to take a pinch of Emma's kitchen confidence and combine it with an ounce of trust that everything will turn out okay. I could even get really carried away with the metaphor and blend in the promise of God's provision and leave it all to rise in the warmth of God's love. Then again . . . maybe I should just get on with the packing.

Sunday, 11 May

This afternoon I persuaded the children to have a go at clearing their bedrooms of junk. The end result of this exercise was three bin bags for the tip and three boxes of 'decent stuff' stored in the garage. I was very impressed with their enthusiasm. They've been so efficient there's hardly anything left! I suspect entrepreneurial instincts are at work: the stuff in the three boxes is intended for a car boot sale and they are expecting to make a fortune. I don't know quite how to tell them that selling half a dozen soft toys and several Polly Pocket accessories will barely cover the cost of the pitch. Perhaps I should just give them the fiver and take it all to a charity shop myself.

This weekend has been a social whirl. In between packing, we have managed to have every meal (except breakfasts) with different sets of friends. The moving date is set for just over two weeks' time, so we are trying to see as many friends as we can before we leave. In the past week alone I have had 'a night out with the girls', a lunch date with a friend and enjoyed several coffee and bun sessions. At the current rate of hospitality, I will have put on a stone by the time we move.

There has been a documentary series on TV recently about people moving home. I have studiously avoided it. When one is actually moving house, one's own traumas are quite enough to be going on with.

Thankfully, our move hasn't been too traumatic, so far. It's just all happening rather quicker than I expected. I feel rather rushed. I don't seem to have a choice about my pace or direction and I feel a bit bruised by the knocks and bumps along the way. Moving house is one of those situations where you are not fully in control, you have to sit back and let events roll you along. This doesn't come easily to control freaks like me. Perhaps I should just relax and allow myself to be carried? Easier said than done.

Monday, 12 May

David left at six o'clock this morning. He is out of the country now for ten days. This means he will get home a mere five days before we hope to move and leaves me juggling solicitors, contracts, mortgage forms, estate agents and removal firms in an attempt to make it all happen.

Tuesday, 13 May

My aura of calm was shattered by this morning's post. I received the surveyor's report on the house we are trying to buy. We knew it would be bad, but we didn't expect it to be this bad. The house has been valued at £2,000 less than we have offered to pay for it and the work that needs doing has been estimated at £4,000 more than we'd budgeted. We're going to have to negotiate a lower price. The surveyor also suggested we employ a panel of experts to check out the details so I have sent in the first one on his list: the gas man.

Thursday, 15 May

The gas man rang me back today; he's had some bother getting the keys but he hopes to get into the house tomorrow.

Saturday, 17 May – far too early in the morning

I've been awake half the night thinking about how I can turn Matthew into an alien; not in fact a malicious speculation on my part but an effort at fancy dress. This afternoon he is due to attend a District Beavers' 'Fun Day' and dress is expected to be on a *Star Wars* theme.

I'd like to protest. I am not one of those mummies who can do clever things with egg boxes, fabric and Pritt sticks. I could just about manage Princess Leia but somehow I don't think he'd be keen. He really wants to be a hideous, three-eyed creature from outer space. The fact that I feel like a hideous three-eyed creature from outer space at this time in the morning doesn't help one bit.

My lack of sleep is not solely due to lack of inspiration on the monster front. I still haven't heard from the gas man, and as if buying a house weren't stressful enough, this is also the weekend of the sleep-over event (sleep being an inappropriate name for it). Emma had two friends to sleep over last night and Matthew has three friends for tea tonight and one to stay over. The added responsibility and the fact that David is away combined for a restless night.

This punishing party schedule isn't pure masochism on my part. The kids were promised these events before we move as 'sort-of-birthday-parties'. Their real birthdays are in July but by then we will have moved and they will have new friends, we hope. They both requested 'sort-of' birthday cakes for their 'sort-of' parties, so yesterday I made a round cake covered in marshmallows which was supposed to be an igloo but looked more like a deep-frozen hedgehog. Today I am going to turn out a medieval castle, complete with battlements (it's next on my list after 'create alien').

A little more sleep would have helped. I read this week that one hour spent floating in a dark tank full of salt water is the equivalent of six hours' sleep. This sounds an efficient if rather unappealing way of getting one's daily rest requirement. I wonder if having a bath with the lights out would have the same effect? I must remember to try it some time; I'd better add it to my list.

Now, what about this alien outfit? Perhaps if I dress him in green (aliens are always green), paint a third eye on his forehead and gel his hair into spikes . . .

Sunday, 18 May

I slept better last night. Matthew and his friend who slept over had both been aliens all afternoon at the Beaver event, so thankfully they fell asleep almost as soon as I'd put them to bed. (They were a bit disappointed about this in the morning but they cheered up when I told them they could have their midnight feast for breakfast.)

It also helped that I wasn't alone. Gran came yesterday to keep me company while David is away. She's also going to hold the fort at home for me tomorrow while I go up to our new house for the day. I feel I need to see it again and reconsider it in the light of this dreadful survey; I might even be able to meet the gas man there. I also want to get the choice of school settled in my mind. I spoke to

'They had both been aliens all afternoon'

the children about the school decision this morning and Matthew wasn't interested. I hope this is due to indifference, not anxiety. Emma, on the other hand, was very interested so I've decided to take her with me.

Monday, 19 May

We saw four schools and one house, but no gas man. Not bad going for a day trip. We even had time to browse round some shops, have lunch in a cafe and be home in time for a late tea. Emma relished being involved in such a grown-up decision, and thankfully our opinions about the schools concurred. We only had appointments at three schools but I quickly realised that my own favourite was the one in Shawcross which I'd already seen, so we quickly arranged for her to see it as well. She liked it too, so that's another decision taken. It's just so disappointing to have found a school and a church in the one location and not to be able to find a house in the same place.

We sat for half an hour on the doorstep of the house we are trying to buy, waiting for the gas man who never came.

Wednesday, 21 May

At last, the gas man calleth! He got into the house

yesterday after we'd left and called me this morning to pronounce the central heating system dead. The boiler is, somewhat alarmingly, under the floor of one of the bedrooms and ought to be condemned. He refused to be drawn about the state of the radiators but hinted that they were also pretty suspect. The whole system would cost at least £2,000 to put right.

David is still out of the country. In his absence I decided to apply the brakes to this house purchase and rang the agent to say we'll have to renegotiate the price and 'Can you wait till Saturday when David will be back?'

Friday, 23 May

I didn't know what to tell the children this morning. Up until the middle of this week we were moving some time next week to a house they'd already seen. Now I have no idea where we will go, or when we will go there. I've put the removal firm on hold and warned the agent we need to reconsider. David flies home today but will need at least twelve hours to re-orientate himself to 'planet family' before we can make a decision. Meanwhile, it's half-term next week so the children wanted to know today if this is their last day at school here, and I just didn't know what to say. In the end I told them, 'Yes, clear out your desks, bring home your PE kit, say goodbye to your friends,' on the basis that even if we don't move next week surely we'll move the week after.

Saturday, 24 May

Everything changed so fast this morning I'm still in shock. David decided that we would ask the sellers to reduce the price of the house to take into account the cost of replacing the central heating system. If they didn't agree to this then, because of all our other misgivings, we said we'd have to pull out. The deal seemed reasonable and we expected them to agree. Even the agent thought it was a reasonable request, but the sellers didn't. They told the agent their feelings on the matter in no uncertain terms and the poor man sounded so shaken I felt sorry that we had to disappoint him. Pulling out of the purchase had not been an empty threat, it was our only option in the circumstances.

We sat in shock for ten minutes before one of us said, 'What the heck are we going to do now?' Or words to that effect. It wasn't a pleasant prospect, having to move out of one house and having nowhere to move into. Our first idea was to ring and ask about rented houses in Shawcross.

'One's become available just this week,' said the man in the agency. 'Unfurnished, empty, three bedrooms, available now, three-month let . . .' It sounded ideal. David has arranged to go and see it on Monday.

Next we called the bank manager, to say, 'Yah boo sucks, your mortgage stinks, we don't want it any more' (or words to that effect). Actually it was just as well that David made the call and didn't use words to that effect at all, because he got a very sympathetic advisor who said, 'Penalty, what penalty? So long as you buy again in three months' time, you won't have to pay a thing.'

Stunned silence.

Suddenly Plan A is out the window and all the obstacles to Plan B are flat on the floor.

'Plan B it is then,' said David. It's taken me the whole day to re-focus.

Sunday, 25 May

This morning at church we told everyone who had thought we were moving into 'the dump' next week that we weren't any more. Their reaction was amazing.

'Oh, I'm so pleased, I thought it sounded awful.'

'I *really* felt it was the wrong place for you.'

'I'm so pleased you've changed your mind,' and so on. The gist of everyone's response was that they'd all felt we'd been buying the wrong house but no one had had the nerve to say so. I don't know whether to feel pleased and relieved that we hadn't gone full steam ahead into a decision that all our friends had agreed (among themselves) was a complete disaster, or to feel annoyed that no one thought to tell us we were making a big mistake. On balance I'm pleased they held their counsel and simply prayed that we'd work it out for ourselves. It's an awesome thing to step in and tell someone else how to run their lives; I'm glad none of them tried.

I only hope that in all their relief that we haven't bought the wrong house, some of them actually notice that at the moment we don't have anywhere to live this time next week. All sold up and nowhere to go is rather awkward, not least because our 'farewell season' is still in full swing. The house is awash with cards and the fridge overflows with left-overs from our latest leaving do.

Moving day, which was meant to be in a week's time, now looks like being the week after next and if I'm still here in two weeks' time I feel I shall have to go round with a paper bag on my head. Either that or we'll have to hold another party; perhaps we'll call it the 'We're Really Leaving Now' do.

Monday, 26 June

Before David left early this morning we made a list of all the questions to ask about the rented place he's going to see this evening. Top of the list was 'Will the owner allow a dog?' It dawned on us yesterday that not all landlords allow pets. We've only had Chester six months; it would be awful for the kids if we had to move without him.

David rang after tea and 'yes, she takes dogs' was one of the first things he said. He'd met the landlady at the property and sounded absolutely delighted. This is all good news. Then I had to tell him the bad news that our agents were having difficulty contacting our buyer. They've been leaving messages for the last few days and getting no reply.

There's never a moment's peace in a house move. Just when you think you've found somewhere to live, your buyer disappears.

Tuesday, 27 May

Still no sign of the buyer. The agent can't understand, she's been so reliable all along. If we're going to move at the end of this week we need her signature and we need it now.

Wednesday, 28 May

Still no buyer.

Thursday, 29 May

I'd just about reached the point of admitting we

were about to go back to square one (i.e. no buyer, no house move) when the agents rang to say they'd heard from her. The poor woman had been in a car accident at the weekend and had only just been discharged from hospital. I felt terrible and immediately repented of all the dreadful things I'd been thinking about her for the last three days. I've also been praying fervently for her speedy return to health and house-buying. Whether or not we move next week or not depends on the outcome of those prayers.

Saturday, 31 May

The children want to know if they are going back to their old school on Monday. I think not, it can only be a matter of a week before we go, but David thinks it could be longer and they should go back to school. This issue, combined with all the accumulated tension of the last few weeks, has simmered between us all day. David wisely took himself to the far end of the garden and took the shed to pieces ready for the move.

Sunday, 1 June

This morning was our last morning at church. I decided before we went that it would be our last, even if we are still here in a week's time. I don't think I can face any more goodbyes. David emptied the loft this afternoon. The children are not going back to school tomorrow.

Monday, 2 June

All my memories are neatly stacked in boxes in our hall. Now my whole life passes before me every time I walk from the study to the kitchen. Each box has a label: 'college notes', 'year abroad', 'love letters', 'wedding dress', 'baby clothes'. It's all there, in faded detail: the life and times of one Sheila Bridge.

This collection of boxed memories has moved five times so far since we've been married. Each time it comes out of one loft and goes straight into another, barely seeing the light of day in between. When it came down from the loft yesterday David wanted to take the whole collection to the tip but I pleaded for a few days' grace. I couldn't bear to let them go without one last sift through to save the really precious stuff. I've promised to reduce it all down to a mere three boxes, and it's not going to be easy. This evening I opened the 'wedding dress' box and tried on the contents. It almost fitted! I felt twenty-one again.

Next I opened up the box with all my old school books. Emma enjoyed looking through these, especially when she discovered that my spelling was once as bad as hers – 'Worse!' she declared with glee.

Spelling was something we worked on this morning during our two hours of 'home school'. I don't think they learnt much, but at least it gave some semblance of normality to the day and made us feel that we were doing something other than just waiting.

Tuesday, 3 June

David left for the north again this morning. This week he is away until Friday, which means that on Thursday we will share our birthday, as usual, but not our location. He will be 150 miles away in Lancashire, poor lad. At least he'll have a present to open; I tucked it into his bag before he left. What with all the expenses of moving we had decided not to get each other presents this year, but then I came down with 'lack of romance' symptoms which could only be cured by the prospect of a surprise pressie so I hope he's remembered to leave one with the kids.

The best present of all would be to move by the end of this week. I'm optimistic; David is doubtful. We'll just have to wait and see. The wise man in Ecclesiastes says there is a time for everything, so presumably there must be a time to move and a time to stay. I hope this is a time to move but every so often I cave in under a pile of anxieties labelled 'Irrational, Absurd and Unlikely': maybe I'll be run over by a bus tomorrow, maybe David will get another job somewhere else before we even follow him to this one, or maybe our buyer is having second thoughts and will pull out, and so on. Philippians 4:6 has been a good antidote: 'Do not be anxious about anything.' It's such a simple instruction, but not too simple. At a time like this I couldn't handle a complicated formula. The simplicity of letting my Father know our needs has become a daily reality, the fact of his Sovereignty a stabilising force.

Friday, 6 June

Yesterday was my birthday and boy, did I know it. The day was okay. I took the kids to an open-air pool and luxuriated in the peace and quiet while everyone else was at school, but as soon as we came home for the evening all hell broke loose. The answerphone had taken seven messages while we'd been out and I had only just finished dealing with those when it was time to cook tea. The phone continued to ring non-stop, partly because an advert for our rabbit hutch had gone into the paper one week later than it was supposed to. In between enquiries about the hutch at least eight callers wished me a happy birthday. This was very kind of them, but by the fifth rendition of 'Happy Birthday to You' my

'It's hard to sound polite when you can see your sausages going up in smoke'

appreciation was wearing thin. It's hard to sound polite when you can see your sausages going up in smoke. ('And what did you have for your birthday?' 'Indigestion.')

The answerphone took three more calls while we ate our tea. Two of these were enquiries about the hutch, which I could have sold ten times over. As it was I virtually gave it away to the first couple who came to see it in the early part of the evening. They were closely followed by three more visitors of the 'Happy Birthday' variety, two of whom got cups of tea and something approaching a chat. In between all this hospitality, the smoke alarm sounding, the phone ringing and the door bell going, I also had two arguments (one with each child, just to keep things even), lost a contact lens and decided to move north this weekend.

I realise this was a risky decision made on the run. Our buyer is still convalescing in an unknown location and has not yet exchanged contracts with us, but I'm worried that if we don't go soon we might lose the rented place we have lined up. I also took this decision alone. David hadn't even called. He was too busy having a great birthday offering corporate hospitality to some clients: go-karting followed by a decent meal. What a drag, eh? And he didn't even leave me a present.

The disparity in our situations wasn't lost on me, and resentment probably had a lot to do with my impulse decision to move as soon as humanly possible. So yesterday I told everyone who asked that we were moving this Saturday, signed contract or no signed contract. But by lunchtime today this plan had fallen through. As I was about to confirm my booking for the removal van for Saturday, I prayed that God would stop me if I was making a mistake, and he did. The removal people had given our slot to someone else who'd confirmed their booking, and now they can't move us until next Thursday so I've booked it for then.

Panic prayers at the last moment are probably not the best way to discern divine guidance but with two children around me all day every day, I'm not getting much time for contemplation or reflection. Listening to God is all very well on a good day, but on a day like today I simply can't hear him; there is too much interference, all of it generated by my anxiety, crackling along our lines of communication. I'm holding on to the hope that, just because I can't hear him, that doesn't mean to say he's not there.

Saturday, 7 June

This morning began with a call from our estate agent. Our buyer has recovered and returned home (thank you, Lord) and is ready to sign the contract (hooray) but (there's always a but) she's decided that as well as the house, she'd rather like to have the shed at the end of the garden. Yes, that's right, the shed that David dismantled last Saturday. Either that, or could she have several hundred pounds off the price of the house, please?

I gave her the shed but on one condition: that she sign the contract on Monday. I then had to break it to David that he had to re-erect the shed he'd spent most of last Saturday taking down.

He was tempted to leave it 'flat-packed'. In fact that was one of his milder suggestions; re-erecting it over the pond was also considered. In the end he put it back up in its original place. We don't even know if we'll need a shed in our new place so leaving it behind will be no great loss and will be worth it if she signs that contract soon.

Monday, 9 June

Having the children around all the time is driving me barmy. They create so many interruptions it's impossible to think in a straight line, let alone pray. Home school is getting to be a bit of a drag and we've only been going a week. I don't know why anybody does this full-time and from choice.

Two weeks ago I wrote that if I was still here in a fortnight's time I'd have to go round with a paper bag on my head. I'm currently looking for one to fit.

Tuesday, 10 June

At last, a little time this evening to myself. David is away this week till Thursday evening. The removal men come on Thursday and load up most of our belongings and pack the last few things on Friday morning before the long drive north. The contract still isn't signed but they are promising it will be; it really looks as if we've got a green light this time.

Just thinking about all the hassle and anxiety of the last few months makes me feel tired. Hebrews 12 possibly isn't the best thing to read when you are feeling emotionally drained and spiritually tired, but I read it anyway because it's familiar. When I got to the bit about throwing off all that hinders and running with perseverance the race marked out for us, I asked God to draw a line under the last few weeks (or put a full stop or turn the page, whatever he prefers). I need a new start spiritually, not just geographically.

Thursday, 12 June

The removal men arrived early and worked remarkably fast. By lunchtime most of the downstairs was empty. By 3.00 p.m. they had cleared the bedrooms of all but mattresses for us to sleep on tonight. It felt good to finally be on the way but nerve-racking too: at the start of the day the contract still wasn't signed.

Four o'clock: the phone rings, the solicitor tells me that the contract has now been signed and we are clear to move. I point out to him that as most of our possessions are already on the van this news comes as a considerable relief. I put down the phone and try to kid the removal men that the sale's fallen through and they'll have to unload the van, but they don't fall for it. I must have looked too pleased. What a relief.

Sunday, 15 June

The last night in our old house was a strange experience. Sleeping on a mattress in a totally empty house, it was hardly surprising I woke early and was ready to be off by half eight. The plan was for me to leave first because I was driving my 'tin can' and David would follow the van up in his company car. The expectation was that they would both overtake me somewhere en route, so if I broke down they would know. The children, who had to be divided between us, drew lots. Matthew drew the short straw and got a seat with me and the dog in my car while Emma and her gerbil went in comfort with David.

Before I left I went for one last wander around the empty rooms, and each one brought back a memory.

In Matthew's room I remembered how he'd still been in a cot when we arrived. In Emma's room I recalled our first attempts at wallpapering. Downstairs I remembered the birthday parties, the dinner parties and so many comfortable conversations over a cup of coffee with friends in the kitchen. Finally I went into the lounge and found that Matthew had left a handmade card on the mantelpiece.

'Hello lady,' it said in large letters on the front, addressing itself to the new occupant of the house. And on the inside, 'Welcome to the house of wonders!'

Oh dear, that brought the hanky out.

Amazingly enough Matthew didn't seem at all distressed to be driven away from the only house he remembered, so once we got on to the motorway I put my foot down. This didn't make any difference because the car only hits fifty-five on a good day, but even so we made it to Shawcross ahead of the van and found our way to a house that neither of us had ever seen before.

The landlady met us at the door. She lives in the basement and we are renting the top three storeys of her house. The ceilings dip in the middle, the stairs are narrow and the floors are creaky, but it's wonderful, exactly what we needed at the very moment we needed it. God is good!

The removal men took one look at the house and headed for the chip shop, complaining loudly about the three sets of stairs. Fortified, they returned and had the van unloaded by three o'clock. We waved them off and surveyed our surroundings. The house is huge. The children have an attic each on the top floor. David and I are on the second floor near the lounge and the bathroom, and the kitchen is on the first floor. The kitchen is enormous, which is just as well because the sofa and comfy chair were too big to go up the narrow stairs to the lounge. The piano is also in the kitchen, which has a certain timeless quality about it because I haven't found our clock yet. My plan was to unpack only the essentials yesterday; I thought I had everything out I needed until Emma washed her hair this evening, when I suddenly appreciated the necessity of a hair dryer. I had to open four more boxes before I found it.

These first few days have been an assault on our senses. I heard the village clock chime until three on the first night, kept awake by all the unfamiliar noises. Yesterday morning, before we started unpacking, we made it out to get our bearings and discovered that our location is a feast for the eyes: steep green hills, spreads of moorland, dramatic rocky outcrops. This is the kind of place we come to on holiday, so in another week's time I'll be expecting to go 'home'.

On our second morning we woke to a delicious smell: the landlady cooking her breakfast in her basement kitchen. The children were disappointed it wasn't theirs.

'It's for the lady in the sewers,' Matthew explained to the dog. (He meant 'cellars'.)

Before the end of school on Friday I took the children up there so that they could meet their teachers before they start tomorrow. They were impressed to find some post waiting for them, a card from their old head teacher, and seemed quite relaxed about the visit. I hope they get on okay tomorrow.

Monday, 16 June

They got on fine at school. I was more nervous than they were. Matthew came home and started a letter to a friend reporting that he'd 'made two fiends already'! He's even arranged for one of the fiends to come round and play.

I enjoyed the peace and quiet all day. In the space created by being removed from everything that has occupied and preoccupied for weeks, I hope I will be able to at last sense again the presence of God.

Tuesday, 17 June

I feel so self-conscious in the playground. I only have to say 'Good morning' and it's obvious I'm not from round here. This morning, however, I was bowled over by the friendliness of one parent I had already met in church on Sunday.

'Come and have a coffee,' she said. Not tomorrow or the next day or a week on Thursday but now – how wonderful!

I was so delighted by her friendliness that we chatted all the way back to her house and I was halfway through a cup of coffee before I remembered I'd left the dog, ten minutes away, tied up outside school. Whoops. There was good reason to be engrossed, however, because my new friend was not being simply friendly. She knew we wanted to buy a house in the village and she was offering us hers!

I couldn't quite believe my ears and nor could David when I told him at teatime. (It's such a novelty having him come home every night from work.) We've arranged to go back and look at it together on Thursday.

Thursday, 19 June

We spent about half an hour looking round Pauline's home. It's not as straightforward a decision as it first appeared. As it is at the moment it's too small, so we need to work out if we can afford to extend it. Part of me wants to buy it just because someone so friendly wants to sell it, but I know I've got to be more logical than that. David also felt he needed to pause and consider the decision. I think both of us feel nervous after so nearly making a disaster of a decision over the last house. I read an Eddie Askew poem this morning that just seemed to sum me up at the moment.

> Lord if it's the weak you want
> the foolish,
> then I'm the one.
> Well qualified in weakness,
> Post-graduate in foolishness
> No other qualities but those
> And a glimmer of faith.
> Weak like the rest
> For you to use.
> You'll need a miracle a day
> to keep me going,
> But if anyone can do it Lord,
> You can.

(From *Facing the Storm* by Eddie Askew, published by the Leprosy Mission)

Saturday, 21 June

What was that about 'a miracle a day'? This morning we discovered yet another house in our price range available for sale in the street of our choice. It seems incredibly good timing to have not seen anything we could afford in the village for the last six weeks of looking and then to be given the choice of two in the first week we arrive.

But having a choice also complicates the decision. We went back twice today to see the second house that's come up. David feels it's ideal even though we'd still have to extend it. I have to agree but I hate to let the first person down.

Sunday, 22 June

It may be mid-summer but sunny it isn't. It's rained every day this last week and today was no exception. We managed to get out for a walk between showers this afternoon and I tried out the birthday present that David did eventually get round to buying me. Practical as ever, he bought me a pair of walking boots. I have four weeks before the long school holidays and I have resolved to break in my new boots by discovering all the local footpaths. My other resolution is to read; I have felt starved of good books lately and I plan to plunder the library.

Some great news greeted us when we returned from our walk. Becky, David's sister, gave birth to her first child this morning: a girl. After the parents, Matthew seems to be the most pleased by this news because now he is no longer the youngest member of our extended family.

Monday, 23 June

The deed is done. The offer on house number two has been accepted and I have told Pauline that we are not going to buy her house. Ungrateful child that I am, I have sulked for twenty-four hours over this decision. Whichever house we had bought would have needed an extension. Having just lived through an extension last year I didn't fancy living through another one. Not only would it be a very tight squeeze to get into either house as they stood, but we would then have to put up with all the dust, the mess and disruption of the building work. The idea didn't appeal.

In the middle of this long sulk about not being able to afford a big enough house, our landlady dropped round to say that she no longer needed us out by September, we could stay to January if we needed to. This means that we won't have to move in until the building work is finished. An undeserved and unexpected blessing.

I repented at once of my ingratitude and lack of faith. There remains just one small minor detail to solve: how are we going to pay for this extension?

Tuesday, 24 June

David's been doing some sums and worked out what the new house will cost us, estimating the cost of the extension. His conclusion was that I'll have to make a more concrete contribution to family life.

'More concrete than ironing, cooking, cleaning and shopping, you mean?' I replied.

Wednesday, 25 June

It's still raining. I didn't want to get drenched so I stayed in this morning and got bored. So bored I decided to bake. I have to be bored to bake. Anyway it paid off; it meant I was in at lunchtime when someone knocked at the door. I opened it to find my friend Sarah and her two children come all the way from the Midlands to see me. I was amazed. So was she. She had set off without an address, knowing only the name of the village. That's typical Sarah. Thankfully the man in the paper shop recognised her description of me and pointed her in the right direction.

It was great to see her and we tramped around the village in the rain while I showed her the sights.

Friday, 27 June

Sent off my first job application today. I read Matthew 10:30 this morning reminding me that even the hairs on my head are numbered, so God must be a lot better at maths than I am. Even so, pennies directly from heaven to pay for this extension seem unlikely in view of my teaching qualification. I hope that God will open the right door and close the wrong ones.

Saturday, 28 June

I didn't want to go to sleep last night. The night before I'd found myself in attendance at a mass suicide. That was about the third nightmare this week. I know that moving house is like a bereavement but surely my subconscious is taking it too far. I think it's just the toxic combination of isolation and anxiety; David prayed for me last night and I had an undisturbed night.

Sunday, 29 June

I have just enjoyed a delightful return visit to early motherhood, and boy am I glad to come home. We spent today visiting my sister-in-law and her husband, whose first baby was born this time last week.

We took the scenic route over the hills which made us all feel thoroughly nauseous: memories of early pregnancy. Only the dog was actually sick but someone (guess who?) still had to clear it up (clearing up messes being one of the essential skills of motherhood).

The dog recovered and the long drive was well

worth it. The baby was beautiful, my children were impressed, the father was proud and the new mother wavered precariously between tearful exhaustion and tearful elation. There is no experience quite so overwhelming as that first week of parenthood. The responsibility seems so enormous. The baby's every burp and bowel movement is a possible cause of wonder or anxiety. There seem to be hazards at every turn: is she too hot? Is she too cold? Is she still hungry? Has she got wind?

It's a bit like being sent on a desperately important mission in a completely foreign country without so much as a map or a phrase book. Other people can tell you they've been there, they can even give you guidelines about the best route to follow, but at two in the morning, when you and the baby seem to be the only people awake in the world, you have to find your own way through.

I remember feeling very desolate in those lonely night hours. When I really felt I couldn't cope any more I used to walk out of the door, take a deep breath, tell myself I was the midwife and walk back in again with all the borrowed confidence of a good actress. It didn't always work but it made me feel a little better. With the benefit of hindsight I can see that it was in fact in those worst moments, when I felt I must be failing, that I was actually learning: learning to trust my own instincts, learning the language of my baby's needs and discovering my own unique potential for meeting them.

That's not a bad parable for my current experience: moving long distance. When it feels that we are floundering so much that we will surely drown, perhaps that is the moment we are actually learning to swim.

I have missed many close friends this week and the days have started to drag. I have been swayed by irrational fears. I have felt overwhelmed by all the changes in my life. But being overwhelmed is a necessary precursor to faith. I do not have to drown; the whole point of the exercise is learning to swim.

Monday, 30 June

Grandma and Grandpa Bill came to see us today. They were on their way home from a holiday in Scotland and this was their first visit here. I had hoped it would stop raining for them. But it didn't. Still, in spite of the drizzle they seemed to like the place and it was good to see them. They went on their way after tea, having seen the children after school.

Wednesday, 2 July

Wednesday again. It seems to be lowest point of each week. I am managing to fill up my time reasonably well with reading, writing letters and walking the dog. I have even started to knit a school jumper for Matthew, but by Wednesday afternoons I get to feel sorry for myself: all this activity and I'm still only halfway through to the next weekend.

The walk to school and back with the kids is the social highlight of the day. But sometimes I feel like an intruder in the playground among the groups of women who have stood and conversed comfortably together every day since their children started school. It takes an effort to start a conversation, and as soon as I do my obvious lack of local accent makes me feel conspicuous.

This afternoon, though, I had a surprise. I was just standing quietly on my own in the playground when Frank and Mary, our old next-door neighbours, walked through the gates. I couldn't have been more surprised or delighted to see them. Having been on holiday further north they had broken their homeward journey to come and find us – what a lovely surprise. The children were also so pleased to see them and chattered non-stop all the way home, filling them in on all our news. We gave them a guided tour of the house and village and a quick cup of tea before they had to go. It lifted all our spirits to see them, even though I can't yet get over the feeling that this is just a temporary situation and in a few weeks' time we'll pack up and go 'home'.

Friday, 4 July

Today I found someone to draw the plans for the extension on our house-to-be. It feels a bit risky forking out money for plans to be drawn up on a house that's not yet ours but we know from experience how long the planning procedure can take and we want to have the permission in time for the work to start as soon as the house is ours. Even though the landlady says we can stay until Christmas we obviously don't want to be paying rent and mortgage for too long.

Saturday, 5 July

We joined a walk today. The church has a walking fellowship group that organises walks and this one was advertised as being suitable for families: just nine miles and one steep ascent in the pouring rain. Mind you, they weren't to blame for the rain. It has rained every day for the last three weeks, in fact every day since the day we arrived. It took me two and a half weeks to recall the prediction about rain that my prayerful friend had given me back in January. Accepting it as a symbol of blessing has made it easier to put up with for the last half a week, but we could have done without it today. About ten of us trudged through the damp countryside and I felt like Jonah every time someone joked about who was to blame for the weather.

Matthew and I gave up halfway round and took a short cut home. We had enjoyed a hot bath and a meal by the time Emma and David returned. The sun came out and the rain dried up as soon as they entered the house.

Sunday, 6 July

Walking again today, but not in the rain, thankfully. The school had a short sponsored walk organised for this afternoon and I went along with the kids. Everyone had called it the 'POP' walk but for the life of me I couldn't figure out why. Was it the Parents and Other People walk? The Plebs or Paupers walk? Maybe even the Particularly Outrageous Pedestrians walk? (It was fancy dress, after all.) It was none of the above. Instead it was the juvenile equivalent of the 'beer walk', a local charity walk between pubs. Our event was a charity walk between specially provided fizzy pop stops, hence 'Pop Walk'. I wish someone had told me; I'd taken several litres of liquid in the rucksack.

Tuesday, 8 July

'She hit me!'
  'He's got my pen!'

'She's in *my* room!'

'It's his fault!'

'You always take her side, IT'S NOT FAIR!'

This is a 'sibling rivalry' scene from our own family drama. Unfortunately it's a scene that's been replayed too frequently for my liking in the last few weeks. Perhaps it's just their way of adjusting to all the changes or perhaps it's the absence of other friends to distract them.

Either way, the script always ends with that final stinging accusation about fairness, usually directed at whichever of us is the participating parent. I try not to be the PP if I can possibly help it. It is a self-defeating task to step in and pass judgment over whatever item or privilege is in dispute: the winning child will be triumphant, the loser will feel rejected, hard done by and even unloved, and the parent will be unpopular.

Up until now my tactic has been to intervene only if first-aid is required. But it's an exhausting business living with constant low-grade hostility. This week, however, I have found a new way to shorten the sibling rivalry scene. I've found inspiration from one of those American self-help manuals, the type that claim to tell you everything you need to know about whatever it is you most want to know about. This one was about Sibling Rivalry: 'what causes it?' (rather obvious I thought), 'what effects does it have?' and 'what to do about it' (tell me more).

It was very helpful and gave me some great alternative lines for my script. Apparently you are supposed to encourage them to articulate their feelings, e.g. 'You're angry with your brother: say how you feel with words, not fists.' If that line fails (or you arrive on the scene too late) then it's meant to help if you describe what you see, e.g. 'I see a child raising a tennis racquet and another child throwing a lorry!' At this point you add, 'We need a cooling-off period now,' and send them to separate parts of the house, or if you're feeling very brave you will leave the room without intervening in the carnage, saying something along the lines of, 'I'm confident that if you both think about it you will find a way to enjoy your train set together'!

The main theory behind the book was that siblings would get along better if you helped them find constructive ways of expressing their feelings. Taken out of context the type of phrases they suggest you use do sound rather stilted and I've felt very silly saying them, but amazingly enough they've worked. Perhaps they have just been stunned into silence by the change of script, but at least I haven't had to use the 'shut up and go to your room' line for the last three days.

This morning, though, I fell foul of the Romans

'I'm confident that if you both think about it you will find a way to enjoy your train set together!'

7 principle: I did the thing I didn't want to do. It's disappointing to recognise the gap between what you want to say and what you actually say. Knowing the right thing to say is one thing, staying calm enough to actually say it, is another.

Wednesday, 9 July

No 'Wednesday blues' today, nor any unexpected visitors. Instead I had the quote from the architect doing our plans. David is still sweating over the sums and I am applying for jobs. If we are going to buy this house and continue to eat I am going to have to find some kind of employment. I spent today filling in an application form for another part-time teaching post.

Friday, 11 July

Sports day and no rain, what a fortunate combination. The Infants had their races in the morning and the Juniors in the afternoon. This meant that all the mummies like me, who had children in both ends of the school, spent the whole day sitting on the school field. Given that the sun was shining this was quite a pleasant way to spend the day. My only responsibility was to shout myself silly every time one of my children took part – correction, every time Matthew took part. Emma would have disowned me if I'd so much as cheered once. As soon as Matthew's class came on to the field he was looking out for me and we waved enthusiastically at each other for a full five minutes. I waved madly at Emma when she came on the field and she raised an eyebrow in return; public displays of affection have never been her thing. I reined in my enthusiasm as she took off in the cross-country and clapped demurely as she crossed the line. I think I did okay; I hope she'll let me back to watch next year.

Saturday, 12 July

Matthew woke us early this morning. He was excited about our day visit back to our old street, but unfortunately none of us shared his enthusiasm at such an early hour. He was despatched back to bed in no uncertain terms and proceeded to wail about this unfair treatment for a full fifteen minutes, by which time we were all thoroughly awake and thoroughly bad-tempered.

It wasn't a good way to start the day. At least it got better. We were invited to a garden party put on by some of our old neighbours and it was a good chance to see old friends. I had wondered if it was too soon to go back but I'm glad we went. I would have been miserable if I'd missed it.

Wednesday, 16 July

The new lines in my sibling rivalry script are still working; it's been a good week. Mind you, I've hardly seen the kids. Their social life has taken several leaps forward since small friends of the 'playing out' variety have begun to call. This is an innovation for us. Where we lived before, children came round or went out to play only when Mum or Dad had made arrangements for them to do so. It's taking me a little while to get used to the free and easy way that children arrive, depart, and drift in and out of each other's homes, but I think I like it.

I've also been out and about. Today I spent a very wet day in a small market town half an hour's drive away. The only reason for going there was to meet a friend who lives half an hour further on from the same small town. Meeting someone in a place that neither of us had ever been to before was somewhat tricky but worth the effort. It was great to see her and the rain provided an excellent excuse for spending most of our time in tea shops.

Friday, 18 July

The architect rang this morning to say our plans were finished and he'd be sending them off to get planning permission. Everything seems to be moving smoothly. Life isn't normally this straightforward. I ought to just enjoy it but instead it makes me suspicious, like when the children are too quiet upstairs and I know they're up to something. Surveyors, solicitors and banks are all doing their stuff but will not be hurried. David is about to go away on business, so if our previous experience is anything to go by, all the decisions and signatures will be required in his absence.

It was the last day of term today so I made the most of my last chance for unaccompanied shopping. I went in search of a superstore and got hopelessly lost. I did at least find the King of Kings. Not, in fact, a profound encounter with the Almighty, but the name of the town's Christian bookshop. Then I found a cake-maker's shop and, on impulse, I went in and hired two cake tins: a number nine and a number seven shape. I'm gearing up for Birthday Week again: this year they are both having outings instead of parties but a decent cake is still essential. I thought the shaped tins would provide an easy way out.

David is not Mr Popular at the moment, going away for the first two weeks of the school holidays and missing both the children's birthdays. I know it's not his fault but that thought doesn't help much in situations where I badly need another pair of hands, birthday outings being a case in point. We are bowling on Emma's birthday and skiing on

Matthew's (as you do, in the middle of summer). If I make it through both events without a visit to casualty I'll be content.

Saturday, 19 July

I baked the number nine cake last night and it sank conveniently in the middle. I hope I do better with the next one, there isn't anywhere convenient for a number seven to sink.

Wednesday, 23 July

The early mornings have been busy this week, too busy by half. Monday, Emma's birthday, began at 4.50 a.m. She came in to ask if it was time to open her presents yet and was sent straight back to bed without so much as a 'Happy Birthday to You'. When she reappeared at 6.20, I was a little more accommodating.

Birthdays begin with the ritual opening of presents on our bed. Emma's main gift was an electronic personal organiser which has since been re-named the 'figital digital'. Smaller than a pocket calculator, this little gizmo promised to store three hundred names and addresses, several hundred memos and diary dates, as well as tell you the time in Outer Mongolia (in case you wanted to know). All this and a secret message facility to boot; Emma was well impressed. The one small obstacle in the way of all this dazzling technology was the fact that someone had to programme the wretched thing and that someone was me, David having left the country twelve hours earlier.

Regretting the fact that I hadn't got him to programme it before he left, I found myself attempting this task at barely 6.30 a.m. The instructions may as well have been in Japanese for all the help they offered but, by teatime, we'd done it, we'd mastered all eight functions, even the metric conversion facility, and we were very pleased with ourselves.

On Tuesday the children let me have a lie-in to make up for our early start on Monday. Matthew got up at seven and made a solo attempt on breakfast. He laid the table, made place cards, put the cereal in the bowls, added the milk and then sat down to read a book for half an hour before calling me to my bowl of warm, congealed Shreddies. How thoughtful!

This morning I was up early to get the shopping done. Tomorrow we are off to visit a friend for a few days so I needed to get all the stuff in ready for the next birthday. Finally got through to David this evening on the phone. On Monday evening I'd spent over an hour writing him a long chatty e-mail telling him all about Emma's birthday. I felt sorry for him missing out, so I had tried to give him an entertaining account of the day. Then I lost the whole message somewhere in the computer when I logged on. I typed a second, much shorter, somewhat terse account and sent that off. This evening he tells me he can't get my e-mails, something about having the wrong adaptor. So much for the high-tech age.

Sunday, 27 July

Matthew's birthday, and he woke at 6.50 a.m. I suppose I should be grateful. His main present was a basketball, a delightfully straightforward 'throw it at your sister' type object which required no programming; he was delighted and so was I. His outing is tomorrow. I have booked the three of us on to a two-hour 'taster session' on a local dry ski slope. It was Matthew's choice – well, almost, he originally wanted to go snow-boarding but I managed to persuade him to try straightforward skiing first. I'm rather nervous about the whole idea but it's only for two hours.

This last week went quickly. Going away to a friend's helped. It distracted us from David's absence and the house purchase. We also met my friend's offspring and got to know her husband a bit better. I nearly ruined our attempts to make a good impression on our first morning there. I went to the loo at half six and, half-asleep, somehow I managed to knock a tub of toothbrushes off the edge of the sink while washing my hands. Only my host's toothbrush didn't make it safely to the floor and I had to leave a Post-it note on the mirror saying, 'Sorry, your toothbrush is in the toilet.'

I don't do mornings. David does. My contribution to family life is best made once the epithet 'early' no longer applies to the concept of morning. I'm looking forward to his return tomorrow.

Thursday, 31 July

Monday was ski day! And so was Tuesday and so was Wednesday, but I didn't know that on Monday when we started.

Out of the three of us, I was the only one with any previous experience and I was the only one feeling nervous. Perhaps these two facts were connected. I last skied at the age of five, thirty years ago. This experience didn't help. Within minutes the children were making progress and I was a quivering wreck. After some simple balancing exercises on the nursery slope they (along with the seven other children in the group) moved further up the slope and started on turns. This left me (the solitary adult student) to creatively explore all the varied ways in which one can fall off a pair of skis.

An hour later and I, too, graduated from the nursery slope and started on turns. To my delight I found I could indeed turn left and right, but not in any way I could control. Meanwhile the children were on the slalom course even higher up.

'Never mind, you'll have mastered it by tomorrow,' the instructor shouted down to me.

'Tomorrow? What does he mean, "tomorrow"?'

I quizzed the parents on the sidelines. To my horror I discovered I'd booked us on a three-day intensive course! The kids were delighted. I was appalled; it looked as if this exercise in humility was going to last all week.

Mind you, I did improve on Day 2: I mastered the snowplough (the 'stop' position). You simply do an impression of a chicken laying an egg and you stop. Inelegant but effective. Pride, however, goes before a fall, although in my case it was more of a sprawl. Descending on one's backside down a slope the texture of a scrubbing brush is not to be recommended. I also braked with my thumb, which was even more painful.

Yesterday I sat out with a still throbbing left thumb and watched the children come down from the summit. They made it look so easy: they turned, they swerved, they even smiled! They had balance and poise and one thing missing: fear.

Unlike me, they didn't stop to think, 'It'll hurt if I fall', 'What if I break something?' or 'Am I insured?' They didn't let all the 'what if' worries get in the way of a good time.

How often do I let my 'what if' worries spoil the fun? 'What if the house purchase falls through?', 'What if I don't get a job?', 'What if I am rejected?',

'What if we're making a mistake?' I know I need some help with this issue; I'm still worrying more than I'm trusting. I know 'Perfect love casts out all fear', but I need to be willing to let go of my fears and swing out into life like a child, secure in the safety net of God's love.

We did end up in casualty. My left thumb was really painful and on the last day Emma injured her right thumb in the same way. Two hours, two X-rays and two bandages later, we returned home nursing a pair of sprained thumbs. Nothing broken, thankfully. The experience was worth the risk.

Friday, 1 August

Hooray! Holiday time at last. David finished work today for a week and there is something to look forward to in each of the four weeks left of the school summer holiday. Today it was the arrival of our friends, Jane and David, for the weekend. I'm so glad of company and adult conversation. I feel very detached from the rest of life and being a full-time children's entertainer is doing my head in. I also feel as if life is on hold until we are settled in our own home. I know life is meant to have pockets of time, such as holidays, when normal life comes to a stop, but after two weeks of rest it's reassuring to return to normality. I feel as if I have entered a rather large pocket of time during which all I am required to do is sit on the sidelines and wait. I have left behind the routine that passed for normality in our old home and have no idea what form normality will take up here, nor when it will resume. In the middle of this, it's reassuring to see familiar friends.

Saturday, 2 August

With all the enthusiasm of a first-timer, David spread out the Ordnance Survey map on the kitchen table after breakfast and said, 'We'll climb that hill there.'

And climb it we did. We didn't just reach the top, we walked across the top and down the other side. It took us all day. I think David was working on the theory that if the ascent was steep enough no one would have enough breath to moan. It worked.

Monday, 4 August

Finally finished my third job application this morning. This one is to go on the supply teaching list for our local authority. I heard last week that I didn't get the first job I applied for, but that was no great surprise. I would like to teach in primary schools for a change, but have no experience so doing supply work is one way of building up experience and getting paid for it. Filling in forms is so tedious; if I wrote my name and address once I wrote it a dozen times. There were police forms, health forms, equal opportunity forms – I almost gave up, there was just so much to fill in. Once it was posted the rest of the day was taken up with shopping, packing and ferrying the dog to the kennels in preparation for our few days away in the Lake District.

Friday, 8 August

On Tuesday we climbed Helvellyn. We arrived at 'base camp' just before eight in the morning and had breakfast in the nearest cafe. We had with us two children, a packed lunch, four anoraks and a map. The first seven items were indispensable, the map was superfluous. At least two hundred other people had also chosen to climb Helvellyn that day. The wide path up the side of the mountain was clearly marked out by people in anoraks, a brightly coloured stream of moving blobs.

Five hundred feet up and I, too, was a brightly coloured, melting blob of exhaustion. It hadn't been easy convincing the children that climbing a peak would be an enjoyable way to spend the day, so in spite of aching limbs and a heaving chest, I had to do a passable impression of having a good time.

'Where's the fun in climbing a mountain?' Matthew said.

'For Dad and me, it's the challenge and sense of achievement. For you, it's the Choc Dips at the top.'

'The 'choc dips at the top' ploy worked very well'

The 'Choc Dips at the top' ploy worked very well; the children made it to the summit without a murmur of discontent. If only the same could be said of their mother.

You can't see the top of Helvellyn from the bottom. For the first third, the hill reveals itself to you slowly: you only see fifty yards ahead to the next horizon and then, when you reach that, there's another new horizon to aim for. I was just reflecting on this apt analogy of life (thinking you've arrived and discovering there's more) when we caught our first glimpse of the summit. It seemed a very long way off but turning back was not really an option. Not only was it already a long way down but, due to the operation of a one-way system, any back-tracking would have to be done against the tide of humanity flowing up the mountain.

Phrases from Hebrews 12 came to mind: 'Since we are surrounded by such a great cloud of witnesses . . . throw off everything that . . . entangles . . . run with perseverance . . .' I wasn't inspired to break into a run but I did at least make it to the top, where we ate our lunch along with several hundred others.

The 'crowd of witnesses' had kept me going. In particular it was the old man and the four-year-old boy walking behind me. I know he was four because I asked him when he attempted to overtake me. I was shamed into a faster pace and beat them to lunch at the top.

We took the longer, more leisurely route down the mountain and enjoyed watching a farmer and his dogs rounding up his sheep from right across the hillside. Reaching the car again by four, we drove on to Windermere to look for our B&B. Several hot baths later, we were revived and ready to eat. The landlady suggested a restaurant round the corner and we set off, followed by several other guests clearly dispatched in the same direction.

Eating with young children in any restaurant other than a burger bar can be a nerve-racking experience. It's the long wait for your order that they find difficult. This is because they are blissfully unaware of the time it takes to prepare a meal; as far as they are concerned, meals appear instantly the moment I say, 'Tea's ready' (if only it was that easy). The restaurant we chose soon got very busy and I felt very conscious of the glances from fellow diners. Thankfully the wait wasn't too long and we managed to keep the children cheerful right the way through to dessert.

The following morning when we sat down to breakfast in the guest house I became aware that the single lady sitting at the table next to us was the same single lady who had sat opposite us in the restaurant. This meant she'd had the dubious pleasure of observing our family eat two meals together. When she came over to speak to us at the end of the meal, my heart sank.

'I'd like to congratulate you,' she began (my jaw hit the table) 'on being such a positively interactive family' (dazed expressions all round). 'It's been a pleasure to watch you.' (Does she really mean us?) Feeling the need to apologise in spite of her appreciation, I stammered a few words of self-conscious explanation, but she really hadn't been bothered by the noise, the argument over the tomato sauce or the game of pass the fried egg. 'It's so rare these days,' she concluded, 'to see a family eating and talking together as if they really enjoyed doing so. Such a pleasure, thank you so much,' and with that she left us. We sat in stunned silence for several minutes.

I was very touched – at least I think I was. It dawned on me later that she hadn't actually mentioned 'good manners' or 'quiet well-behaved children' and I did wonder if she was a behavioural psychologist who'd merely enjoyed discovering a peculiar species of family. But no, I'd like to think she was impressed. We spent the rest of the day congratulating ourselves and living up to her praise.

Wednesday saw us at a country park for the day, an old-fashioned place with paddle-boats on the lake and mini-steam trains through the woods. On Thursday the excitement factor went up a notch as we did a big theme park complete with scary rides.

Today we came home and collected the dog, who was very pleased to see us. The rest of the time was spent washing, ironing and sewing on name tapes ready for camp tomorrow.

Sunday, 10 August

Emma safely delivered to camp, minus a pillow, an anorak and a towel. So much for my packing. She borrowed a spare pillow, shared someone's towel and I went back with the anorak when I found it in the boot of the car. Thankfully the campsite is only a few miles from Grandma's, where Matthew and I are staying for this week while Emma is at camp. I am hoping to see some old friends and Matthew is hoping to camp out in the field opposite Grandma's house. David has been left at home and I am hoping he is going to send out some plans to builders. He gets to enjoy the comfort of his own bed at home, I get to spend the nights in a loaned tent with a small boy and seven sheep (the sheep are in the field, not the tent).

Tuesday, 12 August

I put up the tent today and I must have overdone the 'won't this be fun' routine because Grandma volunteered for the first night outdoors.

'Well, if you're sure,' I said, trying not to look too delighted at the prospect of a night inside lest it occur to her that camping out would not be quite the joy I had described. She admitted that she had never before spent a night in a tent, and I assured her it was an unmissable experience.

Come bedtime they made an impressive sight: Grandma floating up the field angelically in her long white nightie at dusk with small grandson in red dressing-gown following behind. They were armed with two torches, a glass of water and a walking stick, which Grandma said was to fend off the sheep. I said I thought a small flock of sheep was very unlikely to mount a hostile assault in the dead of night but she insisted on the stick, just in case any blundered into the tent by mistake.

Wednesday, 13 August

Grandma and Matthew tiptoed in from the tent in the early morning. Matthew had slept well but Grandma hadn't. She'd found a small hole in the tent and was sure she'd heard a small, and presumably determined, fieldmouse attempting to get through it. A dread of fieldmice kept her awake all night. At least the sheep behaved themselves.

Thursday, 14 August

It was my turn in the tent last night. We turned in early before it got dark and fell asleep easily. Around midnight I was woken by a rumble of thunder. I counted the gap between the flash and the crash and got to thirty. Miles away! Nothing to worry about. I rolled over and tried to go back to sleep. Twenty minutes later I was still awake and counting, but only as far as thirteen. It was getting closer: time to abandon ship – or tent, rather.

I have to admit to feeling a bit of a wimp creeping indoors, scared by a few claps of thunder; it wasn't even raining. But given the choice of a comfortable bed under a solid roof or a flimsy tent in a field full of trees, it wasn't a difficult decision. The difficult bit was levering a sleepy boy out of his sleeping-bag, into his trainers and across a field. The full storm didn't hit us until a few hours later, by which time Matthew was once again sound asleep and I felt very relieved to be safely indoors. The thunder and lightning were continuous. I watched from my window in horror as several forks of lightning appeared to come down in the field around our little tent. I read to try and distract myself, a book about angels and heaven which seemed very appropriate in the circumstances, but when the power went off all I could do was to watch and pray. Emma and all the other children were five miles away at camp, sleeping under canvas in a field surrounded by trees. I wondered how many of them would be awake and frightened by the storm. I prayed for the leaders and requested the presence of several legions of angels around the campsite.

Friday, 15 August

It's been a successful week. I've seen several old friends and enjoyed a week away from the pressure of chores. I collect Emma tomorrow.

Saturday, 16 August

The campers all survived the storm. There were no reports of angelic sightings, but fifty safe children and twenty relieved leaders was good enough for me. Emma looked moderately pleased to see me and chatted for the whole of the first two hours on the motorway. As soon as she ran out of things to tell me she fell asleep. The long journey was at least broken up by a stop for lunch at Gran's. Gran has come on home with us and is staying for the coming week.

It wasn't an easy home-coming. The house was a complete tip. At least, it was a tip by my standards – David had promised it would be tidy and it was tidy, by his standards. It wouldn't have mattered so much but this was Gran's first visit. I was irritated. Then I asked how many sets of plans he had sent off to builders, and he hadn't sent any. I was more than irritated. I'd really been hoping to have a builder's quote waiting for me on my return, but the plans hadn't even gone off. I took out my frustration on the tidying and after half an hour of crashing around with the Hoover, muttering under my breath about 'leaving unattended husbands with lists of jobs', I was ready to forgive him. It's hard work sustaining a sulk.

Tuesday, 19 August

Today I met the Academic Board. This fearful-sounding group of people actually consisted of two laymen and a lady vicar, and I met them in a church hall. (Gran was looking after the kids at home.) The purpose of my appointment was to determine how and when I should continue my attempt to be trained as a Reader. A Reader is someone licensed to preach and lead services in the Anglican Church and before we left our old diocese I was halfway through a two-year course. The problem is that up here the course is three years long, and the outcome of today's meeting was the decision that I would need to do the final two years of this course in order to complete my training. All by myself I had decided to take a year out of training anyway, and so the net effect is that having been twelve months off completing I now have three years to go before I'm licensed. It's all a bit dispiriting.

Our relocation was good for David (he enjoys his job), good for the kids (they have adjusted brilliantly) but it feels as if it wasn't good for me. Readership training is yet another aspect of my life that has come to a dead stop. I'm reminded of how I felt a few weeks ago, as if I am holding my breath through a long parenthesis. Perhaps 'life' will start up again when we get into our own home, perhaps it will take longer. But, in fact, life is what is happening right now, or as someone once said, 'Life is what happens to you while you are sitting around planning for what you'd like to happen.'

While I was at Mum's a friend said to me that I should accept this season as a 'time out' on the sidelines, a gift from God, and not get restless. I seem to remember praying for something like this back in June so I ought to be more grateful than I am. As usual my mother summed it up well with one of those motherly maxims, gleaned from goodness knows where: 'Yesterday is history, tomorrow is mystery, today is a gift; maybe that's why they call it the present.'

Thursday, 21 August

The children are suffering from delusions. One of them has believed that a new bike will be arriving any day now and the other is convinced that we are off to the Caribbean for our next holiday. The reality is that we have no holiday booked and they own two perfectly acceptable bikes. They have contracted 'competition-itis'; I think it's a disease caused by too much early morning television.

It's a feverish condition. It comes on suddenly and it is highly contagious, especially between children. Matthew caught it first. He was watching children's television the other morning when he suddenly rushed out of the lounge, clutching a piece of paper on which he had scribbled a phone number.

'I've got to phone this number *now* because I know the answer,' he announced with great self-importance. I realised a phone-in competition had been announced.

'One and a half million other children also know the correct answer,' I replied, trying to put his 'brilliance' in perspective. He didn't believe me and headed for the phone. 'It costs money to make a call and you'll never get through,' I added, determined to put him off.

Nothing worked.

'No one will ring as quick as me,' he said confidently, picking up the handset. The fact that he'd never made a solo call to anyone in his life, let alone to an answering machine, wasn't going to deter him. I had to intervene. He was expecting to shout his answer down the phone line and receive his prize in the post.

What should I have done? Refuse him the right to use the phone? Flatten his enthusiasm? Or stand back and let him get on with it?

I dithered for a bit, gave him a three-minute lecture on the cost of phone calls (25p in this instance) and tried to describe the odds against winning (tricky when units and tens represent the limits of his mathematical ability). I even appealed to greed by describing in vivid detail all the goodies that 25p could purchase in the sweet shop. It didn't work: he was brimful with optimism, confident he would win. In the end I gave in and rang the number for him. Goodness only knows if 'Gooey' was the right answer but that was the one I recorded in his name.

I had hoped that handing over half his pocket money for a two-minute call would bring him back to reality with a bump but I'd miscalculated the strength of his delusion. Last night he confidently told his dad that he would be winning a new bike in the morning. Needless to say, when the winners were announced this morning, he was pretty depressed.

I felt guilty about his disappointment. I could have spared him but he had to learn the hard way. The sad thing is he hadn't even wanted a new bike before he saw the competition. It seems really unfair to dangle exciting prizes in front of children's noses when their chances of winning are so slim.

But not all competitions are down to chance. Yesterday Emma found one that required a modicum of skill. It was a 'Design a Poster Competition' with a prize of a family holiday on a coral island, something well beyond her wildest dreams and our income. Bless her, she really wanted to win it for us and did her very best for a full half-hour with pencils and crayons.

Again I felt uneasy. Should I allow her to enter? Weren't we just courting disappointment? But then disappointment is a good teacher; maybe she will learn that if she really wants something she has to work for it, not wish for it. Mind you, her current earning potential isn't quite going to stretch to holidays on a coral island. She gets 50p a week pocket money and the opportunity to double that by completing a range of chores at 3p a time.

The chore system has worked well. It's better than nagging them to do simple things like lay and clear the table. Now they not only lay and clear for me but they also Hoover their rooms, empty their bins, practise the piano and clean out the gerbil. Sometimes I can't decide if I'm getting a good deal or if I should have expected them to do these things out of the goodness of their hearts. But as an incentive scheme it works a treat; I only hope these good habits take hold.

My 'work for it' ethic even applies to special offers. Matthew had to work hard for the 'free' toy on the back of the cereal packet and this week he received the fruit of his labours. Every morning for two whole weeks he'd eaten two bowlfuls of chocolate-coated cereal (goodness only knows what it did to his teeth) and he was delighted with the toy when it arrived.

Tomorrow when we go shopping with Gran I have told them they can blow their hard-earned cash on items they have craved: a fishing rod for Matthew and some pens for Emma. Hard-earned pleasures are the best, a cure for competition-itis, I hope.

Saturday, 23 August

We took Gran halfway home this morning. We weren't being mean. We met up with David's sister at the halfway point and handed her over. Having done one week with one set of grandchildren, she moves on to the next. Baby Jennifer might keep her awake at night but is unlikely to be as argumentative as my two have been. During one spectacular row this week I actually stopped the car and hauled the offending child off the back seat in order to have an eyeball to eyeball argument on the pavement. Arguments in cars are the worst sort. I had just got lost and veered across three lanes of traffic, all because of the bad-tempered child on the back seat. There wasn't anything funny about this at the time but I had to laugh afterwards. Gran gave us a few minutes' silence after we got back into the car and then started up a trivial line of conversation as if nothing unusual had happened. Bless her, she deserves an award for non-interference.

After handing Gran over we returned home, to find the air was thick with the sound of sleigh bells, which seemed a little odd given the time of year. Shortly all was revealed: this was Rushcart Weekend, a local festival involving a twenty-foot-high moving haystack and several hundred morris men (hence the sleigh-bell sound).

With bells on their legs, handkerchiefs tied to their belts and huge stacks of wild flowers fixed firmly to their hats, morris men certainly know how to draw attention to themselves. The dog went doolally.

The haystack arrived in the village at around 4.00 p.m. The morris men danced, everyone 'refreshed themselves' in the pub and the whole show moved on to the next village several hours later. Judging from the sound of tinkling bells that lingered well into the evening, several morris men must have missed their haystack home (too much 'refreshment', one presumes). I only hope they found their way to this morning's church service, which was an integral part of the celebration. This was to be closely followed by competitions in wrestling, bad singing and 'gurning' (pulling faces).

For all I know these traditions probably have all sorts of dodgy connotations (fertility rites, etc.) but putting these reservations to one side, I couldn't help being struck by the exuberance of the morris men. With their outlandish outfits and strange traditions it occurred to me that there are some similarities between morris men and clergymen. Not that the wearing of short breeches, yellow tights and flowery hats is typical behaviour for any vicars I know, but morris men and vicars do wear rather strange and out-dated outfits and conduct odd ceremonies – at least, that's the way it must seem to an outsider. Imagine being invited to join in with a ceremony you don't understand, led by people in strange outfits, surrounded by people who all seem to know what they are doing, and you've pretty much summed up the experience of a non-Christian in church.

I asked David, who won't even wear a pink shirt let alone yellow tights, if he harboured any secret desire to don clogs and jig up and down in the street. His reply didn't surprise me. Somehow, I'm relieved.

Monday, 25 August

David left again yesterday. He's away for another week, the last full week of the school holidays. He's been away for three out of the six weeks the children have had off and I have not been best pleased. Tomorrow we are heading back to our old home to stay with friends for a few days and distract ourselves from his absence.

This morning three different builders assured me that they would have quotes waiting for me on my return. The house purchase plods along and we still have only a vague idea of what we hope it will cost. The builder who did our extension last year on our old home has kindly had a look at our plans and told us what he thinks is a reasonable price to look for.

Friday, 29 August

I am *so* glad to be home. My own bed tonight at last. It was great to see so many friends but last night has to qualify as one of the most uncomfortable nights I've ever endured. I'd forgotten to take my own pillow, so after two nights in an unfamiliar bed my neck was really painful. Added to this was the fact that the wind was blowing at precisely the right speed to make something on the roof vibrate very loudly at irregular intervals. The 'something' turned out to be a TV aerial that was just above my bedroom window. By 1.00 a.m. I had picked up my sleeping-bag and walked. I wandered all around the downstairs of the house trying to find somewhere to sleep where I couldn't hear the aerial banging. I opted for the sofa in the living room. It was a compromise for the sake of my neck; I could still hear the noise. I slept (eventually) with my head under the pillow.

At least it's made me appreciate the comforts of home. I wasn't so sad to leave with the prospect of a decent night's sleep ahead of me. I was also hoping the three quotations would have arrived. Two of them had. Both were nearly £10,000 more than we expected and more than we could afford. On top of a sleepless night and a long journey this was a real blow. David isn't even here to share my disappointment or calm my fears.

Sunday, 31 August

David came home yesterday morning having travelled all night. I was going to let him have a shower, a good meal and a nap before breaking the bad news of the quotes. Instead I told him less than three minutes after he stepped through the door. I just couldn't help it. I've been so depressed ever since they arrived. All along we have believed we were following God's directions: we move up here, we sell a house we liked for less than it cost us to buy a house that we don't (well, okay, I will like it once it's extended) and now we find we can't afford to extend it. Even David, usually so cheerful, couldn't think of anything encouraging to say.

We went to church this morning feeling very gloomy, not knowing what to do next. After the service we got into conversation with a woman sitting behind us. It turned out she renovates houses as a side-line and knows just about everything there is to know about local builders, plumbers and electricians. Within minutes she'd written a list of helpful suggestions and contacts and we came home feeling much more encouraged. Perhaps there is a way we can do this after all.

Wednesday, 3 September

September at last! My favourite month of the year. I think I must be odd, few other people share my peculiar preference for this time of year: my sun-loving sister seriously contemplates hibernation, several of my friends feel at a loss all over again as their offspring return to the educational process and serious gardening grannies regret the darker evenings and falling leaves.

Normally I find September very motivating. It is somehow symbolic of moving on in life: starting schools, changing courses, new teachers, new challenges. September has all the freshness of New Year and none of the hangovers from an over-indulgent Christmas.

This year, however, it is only my children who are moving on – both of them have new teachers. I have to admit it was a relief to send them back to school this morning. We've had too much time cooped up together over the long school holiday and we were beginning to get on each other's nerves. Living in a house without a garden has been a real hassle and meant we probably spent too much time indoors.

152

I took the ritual photograph this morning. Every year, on the first day of the new school year, I take a photo of them in their uniforms standing on the doorstep. This year it was a different uniform and a different doorstep. So many changes to get used to but they seem to be coping. My god-daughter starts secondary school today and a godson starts in Reception.

All these milestones are a long way back in my own life but the rhythm of the academic year still affects me. I only have to pass a 'Back to School' display in a shop window and I'm itching to go in for a new pen and a clean pad of paper. This year, however, I'm struggling for motivation. I feel I'm the only one in the family who isn't moving on. Geographically, I moved on in June, and ever since then it has felt as if my life has ground to a halt. I don't have a job to go to, I haven't got a role at church, I'm having a year out from Readership training and I haven't yet got a house to organise. All my vocations, save that of motherhood itself, seem to have disappeared. I feel redundant. I'm impatient to get my teeth into something.

As soon as the house becomes ours I can get stuck into decorating – not that I'm very good at it, but at least it would give me one purpose in life. We expect to complete the purchase within the next week or two, which is also a bit scary because we still don't know if we can afford the extension. Meanwhile the novelty of living in rented accommodation with 70 per cent of our possessions still packed away in boxes has well and truly worn off. I can't wait to get into a place of our own, even if it is too small.

The news from the various builders we've dealt with is unremittingly gloomy: they say the work will take twelve to fifteen weeks, it will cost nothing less than £5,000 more than we can afford and, something we hadn't yet considered, the house will be virtually uninhabitable while the work is being done. The boiler in the garage will be the first thing to come out and the new boiler in the new utility room will be the last thing to go in, so no central heating for the duration of the work. This means we really have to stay here while the work is done whatever the cost. Twelve weeks living in mess and freezing cold does not appeal.

David went away again yesterday morning and he's not back till the end of the week. I hope his absence won't hold up the legal process as we haven't signed anything yet.

Friday, 5 September

I've had three days of minding Emma's cyberpet and it's driving me nuts. I feed it, water it, educate it, discipline it and even play with it before putting it down, and half an hour later it's bleeping, wanting me to do the same thing all over again. I don't know why I ever agreed to this. These toys should come with a health warning for parents: 'Danger: your sanity, your street cred and your sentiments are about to be rearranged'. They make a drum kit seem positively tame.

Emma bought her 'pet' with her own money, in the last week of the holidays. She had spent a long time thinking about it very sensibly before she took the plunge and spent her cash, so it seemed peevish not to let her activate it even if it was three days before the start of term. She hatched it, fed it, watered it and educated it without any help from me. She discovered it needed discipline and play in equal measures and this was a valuable lesson for a nine-year-old who sometimes feels herself to be above the need for discipline. On the last day of the holidays I reviewed my options as to what to do with this electronic beast:

1 All-out cruelty, the 'no, I won't look after it for you' option. This wouldn't do a lot for my popularity but at least I wouldn't be chained to a beeping egg all day.
2 Arrange for it to be 'accidentally' run over by a bus.
3 Remove the batteries.

Number 3 is the most humane.

We agreed that I would look after it while she

was at school only until it died for the first time, and then she could take the batteries out and put it in a drawer until the next holiday. I didn't really know what I was letting myself in for. Dinky (as he is known) has interrupted conversations, cut short outings (because I forgot to take him with me) and rattled my nerves. Thank goodness it's Friday at last; Emma can have the dubious pleasure of his company all weekend. I hope he hurries up and dies soon. We're on Day 6 already – surely he can't last much longer. Listen to me, suddenly 'it' has become a 'he'! Get a grip, woman, this is a micro-chip in a plastic box, not something with a personality.

Monday, 8 September

We've had an unforeseen fatality: Dinky has pegged it. I would like to claim a prize for the most novel method yet discovered to dispose of a cyberpet.

Emma had responsibly 'mothered' it all weekend so by today Dinky was nine days old. Then came the little accident in the bathroom. Dinky fell down the toilet. A real toilet, not a virtual toilet. It was a grisly way to go and Emma was distraught. Desperate measures were required, as were plastic gloves (the things we do for our kids!). I rescued Dinky, David disinfected him and then performed the electronic equivalent of open heart surgery (he took the back off and left him to dry in a warm place).

We don't rate his chances and have tried to prepare her for the worst.

Tuesday, 9 September

Dinky lives! A triumph of endeavour over technology. He fizzled back into life this evening when David reinserted his batteries. Emma was delighted. I wasn't quite so pleased. This is one tough cyberpet and now we're back to Day 1 again. I don't believe it.

I ventured out into village society last night. I spent the evening in the pub. The pub was the venue for the book group I have joined in a bid to get to know a wider group of people than those we are getting to know at church. The group meets once a month and chooses a book which everyone reads, then returns to discuss it the next month before choosing another book, and so on.

I had read this month's book and even taken notes before going along because I was rather nervous about appearing ignorant. Simply going into a strange pub and ordering a drink offered enough scope for social faux pas but I managed it without incident and thoroughly enjoyed the discussion of the book. I only felt stupid when it came to suggestions for the next book to read. My mind went a blank and I couldn't remember the names of any books I'd ever read in my whole life, let alone the names of any authors. For someone with a degree in English this was fairly embarrassing. The other seven people there could list an amazing number of titles, complete with authors and biographical details. I left them to it and simply went along with the final choice.

In the general discussion of daily life which followed this decision, I gleaned the information that only one other person in the group was a parent. No wonder they have so much time to read! I felt a little better.

We went to sign the papers today at the solicitor's. So that's it, as soon as the papers are exchanged there's no going back on our decision to buy the house, extension or not. At the moment all our hopes are pinned on one of the builders recommended by the lady we met at church. He's called 'Vic the Blade', which makes him sound more like a mass murderer than a bricklayer, but he's meant to be very good and not too pricey.

Wednesday, 10 September

Still nothing in the post from the builder and disappointment from the planning office. We should have had our planning permission through by now, so I rang up to ask about the delay. Two of our new neighbours have apparently objected to our plans and so the whole thing will have to go to committee instead of being rubber-stamped. We have just missed last month's committee so we won't get our permission now till next month, some time after 8 October. The planning officer didn't think the objections raised were serious but he couldn't help the delay they had caused.

Great! Now even if we do find a builder we can afford, the chances of him being able to start the second week in October and finish by Christmas seem pretty remote.

I'm trying not to worry about money, and failing. My failure to contribute to the family purse depresses me and limits just about anything I plan to do to cheer myself up. I think we must be mad buying this house in the expectation of finding a builder we can afford.

Thursday, 11 September

Vic the Blade turned in his quote this morning. He was our last hope; we've tried so hard to find someone personally recommended and he was the last one on the list. If we couldn't afford him we didn't know where to turn.

Before the post came I had been reading my Bible, the story of two obscure Old Testament characters going to war against each other. One had God on his side and not many troops and the other one had lots of troops but not God. In true biblical fashion, the one with the smaller army won. This is what I like to hear; I love it when a little guy wins against the odds. I underlined a sentence in my notes, 'Faithful worship and trust in God are of the utmost importance and no amount of human ingenuity can take its place.'

I renewed my resolve to trust God over our situation and bounced downstairs feeling more cheerful. This feeling lasted as long as it took to open the envelope that had come through the door. It was bad news. We couldn't afford the services of Vic the Blade.

It was as much as I could do to get to school with the kids, without dissolving into tears. As soon as I returned home and shut the front door behind me, I crumpled on to the sofa and sobbed. I'd been so hoping he'd be the builder we could afford.

The only thing left to do is to pick someone out of the Yellow Pages, and everyone knows what a minefield that can be.

Friday, 12 September

I sent off two more sets of plans this morning: one to the person we picked out of the Yellow Pages last night, and one to a builder recommended by someone I bumped into yesterday afternoon. My hopes rose slightly with this fortuitous meeting; perhaps this slim circumstance will reveal the way forward.

On the other hand maybe he'll be as expensive as all the others. When you've been disappointed repeatedly it's hard to hope. These two builders are the eighth and ninth we've contacted.

I also realise I'm being a complete bore about this issue; it's all I ever think about at the moment and all I ever talk about. David doesn't seem to be so concerned, but it really distresses me that we might end up living in a house a third smaller than the one we left behind, especially as it took me five years to get that house the way we needed it to be. David's unconcern probably has something to do with the fact that he spends most of his time out of the house rather than cooped up in it, like I do.

All these worries ganged up against me today and beat me to a pulp just before teatime. Why is teatime such a grotty time of the day? It's not teatime itself that's the problem, it's the hour before tea when we are all tired and crabby. David isn't yet home, I'm cooking tea and trying to keep the children from ruining their appetite with biscuits, they are complaining of hunger and asking every five minutes when tea will be ready . . . this evening David came in to find me sobbing over the stove when I should have been slaving over it. Thankfully he had the good sense to take over.

Now, late at night, sitting here with my Bible on one side and my journal on my knee, I pour it all out on to paper. I'm angry, hurt and disappointed. I feel that life 'as I have known it' is over and life 'as it is yet to be' hasn't begun. I'm hanging around in limbo with no home, no job and one single preoccupying passion: finding a builder. If the last few months have been a journey then I have left 'A' and am lost somewhere on the way to 'B'. Being somewhere between where I've come from and where I'm going to is a very uncomfortable place. I really miss 'A' and I'm not sure if I'm going to like 'B'. I thought about the children of Israel on their journey between Egypt and the promised land, how they moaned and longed to go 'home'. I know just how they felt. And how, when they reached the edge of their destination, they still had a river to cross and 'giants' to face: what weak-kneed wimps they were, but how like me. God made a way forward for them; can I believe he'll make a way forward for me? I think about all this but I'm too disheartened to open my Bible and read, too faithless even to pray. Instead I pick up a book of prayers and flick through, not really expecting to find anything that could possibly express how I'm feeling. Then I find this:

Pilgrim God, there is an exodus going on in my life: desert stretches, a vast land of questions.

Inside my head your promises tumble and turn. No pillar of cloud by day or fire by night that I can see. My heart hurts at leaving loved ones and so much of the security I have known. I try to give in to the stretching and the pain. It is hard, God, and I want to be settled, secure, safe and sure. And here I am feeling so full of pilgrim's fear and anxiety.

O God of the journey, lift me up, press me against your cheek. Let your great love hold me and create a deep trust in me. Then set me down, God of the journey; take my hand in yours, and guide me ever so gently across the new territory of my life.

(By Joyce Rupp, taken from *The SPCK Book of Christian Prayer*, SPCK)

I read it through three times in amazement. It's as if the prayer has suddenly appeared in the book just for me. I wonder at the fact that I should happen to pick up this book tonight of all nights, when I've had it for months and hardly ever looked at it. That I should turn to this page and find words that express just how I feel. Perhaps God is near me after all, perhaps he does see into my soul and understand my pain. Thank you, Lord.

Saturday, 13 September

I woke up this morning with the same gloomy mood that had hung over me yesterday. Then I remembered the prayer I discovered. I looked it up again, prayed it again and wrote it out on card for good measure. If I can't pray anything else at the moment, then at least I can pray this one prayer.

I know that I just have to get on with life as it is and not wish myself elsewhere, but I find life 'as it is' a bit depressing at the moment. I'm reminded of an old poster that I've seen stuck up in just about every church hall I've ever visited. When I saw it last week in a corner of our current church hall, its message gave me a sinking feeling of familiarity. The picture is of a spindly flower coming out of some dry, hard ground and the caption reads 'Blossom where you are planted'.

It's not that I object to this pseudo-biblical injunction to 'get on with life, wherever you are', it's just that it's always been said to me whenever I've just been uprooted and repotted elsewhere and, just like plants, recently 'repotted' people are often more inclined to wilt than blossom.

Today at least we were cheered by a visit from a couple of 'hardy perennials': some old friends from two locations ago came in for lunch on their way home from a holiday in the Lake District. They qualify as hardy perennials because they've stuck in one place for most of their lives and have joyfully accepted this as a calling even though they have lived at times through a spiritual desert. During our own 'short-term' calling to that same location, this couple nurtured and inspired us with a cheerfulness that belied their often bleak environment.

It did us good to see them. They were bubbling over with excitement because, after so long in one place, they are finally going to move (not to a new location, only to a new house) and they too are involved with building plans. I was touched by their enthusiasm for the whole moving process but I couldn't share it. I have been repotted, I mean relocated, too many times. Once I finally unpack after this next move, I never want to see another cardboard box in my life (famous last words?).

We took them for a walk around the village and for once it wasn't raining. I poured out my feelings into the safe ears of familiar friends. They listened and said, 'Hmm, that must be hard,' more than was strictly necessary, but it felt good to be heard. The only advice they gave me was to read Exodus. Funny that.

Monday, 15 September

Conversations with new friends tend to go over the same ground. Today I was chatting to someone in the playground and got on to one of my well-worn questions: 'Have you always lived round here?'

Her reply was emphatic: 'Oh, no! I used to live in Hershaw, Kilsworth, Mere and before that in Keresley.' As *all* of these places fall well within my definition of 'round here', I found it hard not to laugh. Here am I, lately of Rugby, previously of Corby, Kent, Cheltenham, Chester and, going back to my childhood, stopping off at all stations to the Far East where I was born. I haven't a clue where I'm from but it's definitely not from 'round here'!

But where I am from is not as important as where I'm going to and where I'm going to has nothing to do with geography and everything to do with theology. It's all about 'running the race': forgetting the past, 'I press on towards the goal to win the prize for which God has called me heavenwards in Christ Jesus' (Philippians 3:14). This is a struggle at the moment, but help me to follow your route for me, Lord, and not resent every turn in the road.

Tuesday, 16 September

The contracts have been exchanged. The house will be ours on Friday. My mood has been a little more upbeat this week. I have resolved to count my blessings: I have two energetic children, a loving husband, a house and several dozen boxes full of possessions. So what if I can't yet live in the house or unpack the possessions?

Meanwhile the children have been back at school

for two weeks and I am still looking for my brain. I put it somewhere at the start of the long school holidays and haven't been able to locate it since. Actually that's not true, it's not my brain that's missing – child care does after all require intelligence – it's the ability to think in the same direction for more than five minutes at a time. I have become so accustomed to the frequent interruptions and changes of tack that characterise my time with the children that I'm left with a butterfly mentality for weeks after they've gone back.

A heavy cold in the first week didn't help. The man in the hardware shop over the road told me that now I live west of the Pennines, this cold would be the first of many: 'It's the damp, you see.' I chose to ignore this doom-laden prediction, a typical northerner's 'tell it like it is' form of encouragement. Clearly, living here, I am going to need an optimistic mind-set and realistic footwear.

Friday, 19 September

Two newsworthy events today. One, Dinky finally passed peacefully away in his sleep. Having survived the trauma of the toilet, he went on to live a happy virtual life and reached the ripe old age of eleven (days). This time he died of natural causes; at least that's what I told Emma as she laid him to rest, minus his batteries, at the back of her drawer.

Two, the house became ours. Its previous occupants spent the day moving out and dropped the keys off with us as they left. After tea we raced off to have our first long look at our future home. It was pretty exciting, even if we're not moving in just yet. Our rent is paid up to the end of this month anyway and we will use the next few weeks to decorate. Matthew's room is pink from floor to ceiling so that'll have to go, and the kitchen could do with a fresh coat of paint. It's a shame we haven't got the builders lined up for Monday but we don't even have planning permission yet, so we'll have to be patient.

Sunday, 21 September

What a long day we had yesterday. David and Emma left early to collect a hired van. They were going back to Rugby for the day to collect all the garden shed and garage stuff that we left behind distributed among friends. Matthew and I were up early to get him ready for his day out with the Beavers. When I signed him up for the Beaver day trip to Blackpool some time last June, it seemed like a good idea. Yesterday morning it felt like a terrible idea. He'd never done such a long trip without me before, and suddenly he was going to do it with a group of people I hardly knew. I'd been worrying about it all week. I very nearly pulled him out of

'He'd never done such a long trip
without me before'

it, but he was looking forward to it so instead I worried. I worried about accidents, about him getting lost, about him being abducted . . . I confess I ran out of things to worry about, but I worried all the same.

I did balance all this worry with a great deal of prayer and I also did my very best to conceal my concern. Even so, come yesterday morning, I was all of a dither. He had address labels in every pocket, small change for a pay phone should he need it (help, I've never even shown him how to use one), two packed meals, three drinks, a bag of sweets and some still warm buns in his back-pack. With two minutes to spare and awash with maternal protectiveness, I even found a vest and made him put it on (I've no idea why I felt the wearing of a vest would help but I was certain it would).

In the event, all was well. I spent the day at the house measuring, planning and cleaning. I didn't know who to worry about the most: Matthew on the coach or Emma and David in the van. In the end I put the radio on and sang loudly. It seemed to help. I hope our new neighbours didn't hear.

I was so pleased when it was finally time to go and fetch him The coach was due in at 8.00 p.m. but I was there by 7.45. And I waited and waited and waited. Thankfully I was not alone; I had all the other parents for company, several of whom had mobile phones. So did the Beaver leaders, so at least we were kept in touch with their slow progress home. Two calls and three hours later the coach finally rolled in at 11.00 p.m. and a very weary Matthew stumbled down the steps. Still laden with his back-pack, he looked pleased to be home. Not as pleased as I was to have him back.

This morning I opened the back-pack. Both meals, one labelled 'lunch' and the other labelled 'tea', lay there untouched. He hadn't eaten a thing for the whole fourteen hours, he was worried about being poorly on the coach. Poor little lad, no wonder he looked pale. He still insists he had a great time 'except for the long time on the bus'.

This evening I called a close friend. She had just delivered her first-born to university. And as I talked to her I realised that all over the country this weekend hundreds of middle-aged mothers are wandering in and out of empty, unusually tidy bedrooms. They are opening their fridges and being surprised at the amount of food still left in them. They are amazed at the floor space suddenly created by the absence of abandoned pairs of size 10 trainers. Most of all, they are perturbed by the silence and are hoping it occurs to a certain someone to 'phone home'.

Oh, what agony it must be to watch your first-born leave the outer reaches of childhood and head off alone towards the great unknown. Letting go isn't easy . . . at any age.

Tuesday, 23 September

I've had a happy few days painting. So far I have done the walls and skirting boards in the study. I'm going to leave the ceiling to David. This evening we went to house group for the first time. I felt a little nervous taking another step that involves me with people but I'm aware I have to push myself into making new friendships. In the event it was fine. We really enjoyed it. Before the end of the evening we explained that we had a house but we needed a builder, and our need was included in the prayers. This morning I read the story of Jairus and his daughter. Jesus dealt so calmly with the situation even though all human hope was gone. He was laughed at when he said the little girl was not dead 'only sleeping' and it reminded me that faith does not laugh cynically. We can only pray and wait in hope.

Wednesday, 24 September

Another quote in the post this morning, this one from the builder we'd plucked out of the Yellow Pages. Astonishingly we can afford him! Just when we'd almost given up hope of ever finding anybody we could ever afford. After all the effort we went to trying to find a builder who was personally recommended, it looks as if we might end up with the guy from the Yellow Pages. Mind you, we'll have to check him out first, I hope he's good and not just cheap.

Friday, 26 September

A morning off from painting today. I went into the children's school to help out. Actually they are helping me more than I am helping them. While I'm waiting to go on the supply list I may as well gain some experience in a primary classroom. Today I was with Year 2 and really quite enjoyed it, which was reassuring.

Monday, 29 September

I'm meeting the builder today at 2.00 p.m. at our house on my own. It's up to me to check him out and decide if we want him to do the work. It's not as if we've got a lot of choice: he's the only one we can afford, but we still don't need a cowboy.

Before then I'm meeting my friend from Sheffield. We're meeting in a country park at a spot equidistant from us both. We've both been relocated recently and it's worth more than half an hour's drive to meet and pray with someone familiar.

Tuesday, 30 September

Praying with Emily really helped. I came home by 2.00 p.m. to find the builder and his mate already waiting for me. I had been praying for divinely inspired intuition but also had some conditions I hoped he'd be able to meet. I wanted him to be able to do the work in eight weeks and start in two weeks' time. This was a pretty tall order; builders usually have work stacked up three months in advance.

I showed him round the house and explained the plans, trying all the time to get the measure of him. But how can you tell if someone's a good builder just by looking at them? It's like buying a car just because you like the colour. Anyway, I did like him. He was pleasant and straightforward, and when I came out with my conditions he replied to each of them, 'That'll be no problem, that,' (a phrase that requires a strong northern accent to be fully appreciated).

So we've employed him. I rang him this evening after talking to David. He starts in two weeks, assuming we get planning permission.

Friday, 3 October

Two weeks of home ownership and I think I have explored all the possibilities offered by a paintbrush:

walls, ceilings, covings, skirtings, radiators, fences . . . you name it and I've painted it. For light relief yesterday I took down the very pink curtains in Matthew's room and threw them in the washing machine with a pot of blue dye. They came out a wonderful shade of blue, an excellent make-over for less than a fiver. While they were drying I pottered in the garden. I won't be able to keep going at this pace but it feels great to finally be doing something towards our home.

Soon all this DIY will have to give way to work of the paid variety, I hope. My application to be a supply teacher ought to be processed soon and the head teacher at the children's school has already promised me some work as a thank you for the all the voluntary time I've been putting in.

Helping in the Infants has been an enlightening experience. Small children are not cynics, which makes them very endearing. They look up at you with trusting eyes and believe every word you say. (Maybe that's one of the reasons Jesus challenged us to 'become like a child'.) This means, of course, that you have to be very careful about what you say. I learnt this the hard way this morning when I was given the task of reading a list of words with each child in turn and then getting that child to read the same list back to me in reverse order. Simon, my first 'customer', brought me his list of words and we read through them together, finishing with the word 'my', at which point I said, 'Now Simon, you read the words backwards.'

Frowning only slightly, Simon looked up at me, looked at the last word on his list and offered, 'Ym?'

I'm going to have to learn to be very precise about my instructions.

In the Juniors Matthew has embarked on a study of what he calls 'Ainshun Eijit' which may sound like an old fool but is in fact a geography/history project. His teacher sent a letter home politely requesting the loan of any artifacts we might have of an ancient Egyptian nature. A little over-optimistic, I thought (the nearest thing we have being a Cretan jug circa 1986), but it made a change from requests for egg-boxes and yogurt pots.

I've been mentally compiling a list of words to use in a letter introducing myself to local head teachers: 'versatile, flexible, diverse, adaptable . . .' 'Egyptologist' hadn't occurred to me. Perhaps I should swot up. One thing is clear: the children won't be the only ones learning in my classroom.

Sunday, 5 October

I've decided I need a minder. Either that or a personal guide. Yesterday I went to London for the day on the train and my personal navigation system failed me completely: I got lost on the way to the station, on the way back from the station and at several points in between.

I was meant to catch the 6.33 from Stalybridge into Manchester, but I missed it. Actually I didn't miss the train, I missed Stalybridge altogether. My mental map of the area failed me and I overshot Stalybridge by several miles and found myself in Ashton-under-Lyme at 6.24, knowing I didn't stand a chance of retracing my route in time for the 6.33 from Stalybridge.

My early morning mind chuntered slowly through my options: (a) give up altogether and go home to bed; (b) drive into Manchester to catch my connection to London; or (c) well, there didn't seem to be an option (c) until it occurred to me that maybe 'my train', the one I was meant to be on, would meander through Ashton on its way into Manchester. Overjoyed at my cleverness, I headed for the station in Ashton.

It was deserted. I spent several forlorn minutes standing on a dark desolate platform hoping against hope that a train to Manchester would suddenly rumble out of the gloomy darkness at the end of the platform. The absence of British Rail staff and any fellow travellers made the prospect seem unlikely.

'Revert to Plan B,' I decided. 'I'll just have to drive into Manchester myself. So what if I've never done it before? So what if I don't have an A-to-Z? So what if it's dark and I've got a train to catch?'

Relying on the same poor sense of direction that had led to my predicament in the first place I set off in hope.

'Never rely on what you think you know,' we are warned in Proverbs 3:5 (if you read the Good News). It later occurred to me that thinking you know where you are going is actually more dangerous than not knowing where you are going. I hadn't got a clue how to get into the centre of Manchester so I paid an admirable degree of attention to signs and I succeeded. If only I'd been as attentive earlier in my journey (there's a sermon point in there somewhere).

After that, the rest of the day was a doddle. I only got lost once in Oxford Street (handy tip: always leave department stores by the same door as you enter) and once on the way back from Manchester in the car, but it was dark by then and I thought I knew the way.

The day was well worth the effort of getting there. It was a day for writers, with a variety of speakers, agents, publishers and the like. I bought a good book on keeping a journal and read it on the way home on the train. It told me I should be keeping a record of my dreams, which I have neglected to do lately so I've resolved to start recording them again. Unfortunately I was so tired after my long day out yesterday I slept like a log all night, so no dreams to report this morning.

Tuesday, 7 October

Spent this morning writing a letter to local head teachers. The point of the letter is to introduce myself as a locally available, ready and willing supply teacher. The tricky bit was trying to sound more confident than I am. Teaching in primary schools is a whole new ball game for me and the idea of only doing the occasional day now and again is to gain experience. I also spent some time on my resources drawer. I need a ready-to-use set of lesson plans that I can pick up and teach at short notice, and it's been quite fun planning theoretical lessons for theoretical children. Teaching real children may not be quite such fun.

What to do with my own children while I teach has been a worry lately. Supply work can be very unpredictable, so I need a very flexible childminder, someone willing to have the children at a moment's notice and preferably not too far away. Someone also willing to have them three days one week and then not at all for the next two weeks. The possibility of finding such a person seemed remote. This evening Matthew's best friend Andrew came to play after school. When Andrew's mum came to collect him, I mentioned my need for a flexible childminder and she told me she was a registered childminder and would be delighted to have them for half an hour before and after school. The fact that she lives four doors away from our new house is a bonus, and this unexpected provision of the kind of help I needed just when I needed it was a real encouragement.

Friday, 10 October

Matthew was up far too early this morning. He had packed his sandwiches, dressed and had breakfast all by 7.15, an hour and a half before we need to leave for school. He then proceeded to nag the rest of us into getting up, washing, dressing and eating. This was an unpleasant taste of my own medicine as the situation is usually the other way round. I think his teacher must have given the class a telling-off about being late and Matthew has taken it to heart, even though we are never late and now he's got this bee in his bonnet about it we never will be. He's just learnt to tell the time, and this may account for his changed approach. Instead of relying on me to tell him what to do, he can work it out for himself, and he also broadcasts his suggestions for the benefit of the rest of the household.

'It's half past seven, time to get up.'

'It's five to eight, you need to eat your breakfast.'

'It's half past eight, coat and shoes on time.'

It's like living with a cross between the speaking clock and a nanny.

Still no dreams to report.

Sunday, 12 October

My sister and family came up yesterday to see us for the first time in our new homes. We were decorating the new house when they arrived and took them back to the rented place for a bite to eat, before going off for a walk. My sister had only taken two steps out of the car before she began muttering about the cold. We had to put the heating on full and find an extra duvet for her bed because it was 'so cold up here in the north'. The fact that the rest of us were fine seemed lost on her.

It was easy to put up an extra four people partly because the place we are renting is so huge and partly because Matthew went to stay overnight with a friend. Before he left I discovered one of his front teeth was tipped at a crazy forty-five-degree angle and told him it would have to come out before he left. A swift extraction was required. We discussed methods and gave it several tentative tugs with a clean tissue to no effect. Matthew was anxious to get it over with.

'Why don't you turn me upside down and drop me on my head?' he suggested gamely.

Thankfully inversion wasn't required: it came out with a quick tug and a twist. He trotted off cheerfully to his friend's house, happy to be reassured that the tooth fairy's visit would be postponed until his return.

'This time he had a choice'

This morning, when he came home, his other front tooth was hanging by a thread. This time he had a choice: the extraction could be performed by his dad, fairly timid and untrained, or his uncle, an experienced father himself and a GP to boot (I know who I'd have gone for).

To my surprise, he requested that his dad do the deed and it was all over in a minute. Both teeth are now under the pillow and Matthew is looking forward to cashing in his crop.

Matthew's choice reminded me of an illustration described colourfully by someone in house group last week.

A small boy stood at the top of a burning building. Two men stood ready to rescue him, one on each side. One was skinny and trembling, 'like a string wi' knots in', and one was brawny and brave, 'wi' muscles in his spit'. Which rescuer would the child choose?

He went to the skinny, trembling one.

Why?

He was his dad.

The two different types of rescuers reminded me of two phoney ideas people often have about God: the 'willing but weak', basically loving and benevolent God who is powerless to do anything. And the 'strong but indifferent' God who is all-powerful and all-knowing but cannot be counted on to care for his creatures. The wonderful thing about God is that he is not only powerful but also loving and kind. But perhaps the point of the illustration is that we trust someone not just because of their qualifications but because of the relationship we have with them. The fact that God is worthy of our trust is as important as the fact that we may call him 'Our Father'.

Monday, 13 October

The builders arrived this morning (the planning permission came on Saturday). We are praying for good weather while the foundations are dug. They cracked on well today. I only went up the once to make the necessary gallon of strong tea, otherwise I left them to it. The best news is that due to a generous 'benefactor' we are going to be able to stay in the rented place until the work is done, which should be by the end of November if the weather is kind.

Tuesday, 14 October

Finally I dream a dream I remember in the morning, and I wish I hadn't bothered! I dreamt I was at some kind of conference and was invited on to the stage to speak. As soon I stood in front of the microphone everyone in the audience got up and walked out! What a nightmare – a psychologist could have a field day with that one, I'm sure. But I can think of a reasonable explanation all by myself: I have two speaking engagements at the end of this week down in London and my subconscious must be getting nervous.

Wednesday, 15 October

Another bad dream last night: this time I was cooking. I dreamt I was mixing up an Instant Whip pudding for the children's tea. I used white spirit and washing-up liquid instead of milk. Thankfully I woke up before they ate it. Too much decorating this time, I think. I don't reckon much to this 'record your dreams' idea.

Sunday, 19 October

I survived the two talks, one on Thursday and one on Friday. To my great relief the audiences didn't walk out as I stood up to speak; in fact they were both very appreciative. The first talk was on parenting and I was just a little unnerved beforehand when I discovered a woman on the front row was a successful mother of ten! I felt a bit feeble having had a mere two and thought perhaps she should do the talk.

Monday, 20 October

The start of Week 2 of building work: the foundations are completed and the walls built up to floor level. The weather has stayed fine and we have been delighted with progress. It's been so exciting to go up to the house every day and see the changes. It's even better to come back home and not have to live in all that mess. What a blessing!

Emma told me this morning that she needed a Roman toga by Thursday. She might have mentioned this over the weekend when I had time to do something about it.

'What on earth for?' I wondered aloud.

'For a Roman picnic, of course.'

Of course. Obvious really, why hadn't I thought of that?

Her class is studying the Romans at the moment. Shame the school don't produce a hand-book for parents; it's not easy making a toga without a pattern and with only the vaguest idea of what one looks like anyway. Emma hunted through her history book for a picture, and in the playground this afternoon I made discreet enquiries among the other mothers. To my dismay, they were enthusiastic: sewing machines, paper patterns . . . even buttonholes got a mention. And there was me, hoping I'd get away with a safety-pin and a bed-sheet. This might be harder than I thought.

Wednesday, 22 October

By this morning I still hadn't made any progress

with the toga. Meanwhile Matthew was feeling vaguely poorly and hoping for a day off school. In the absence of any other symptoms I had decided that he was fit for school and went in at ten to nine to talk to his teacher. Speaking in the kind of code parents use when talking over their offspring's heads, I tried to make his teacher understand that although Matthew was saying he felt sick, I thought it was very unlikely that he would be. His young, newly qualified, 'not yet a parent' teacher didn't seem to understand the code.

'Well, is he sick or isn't he?' she asked.

'Well, neither really, he just thinks he's sick . . .' Honestly, any other parent would have understood.

In the event he wasn't sick, which was just as well, really, because before I'd left the building I'd been employed for the day in Year 2. I knew being a supply teacher would require me to work at short notice, but I had hoped for something longer than three minutes! I had no resources with me and the poor dog was tied up at the school gate. I didn't even know if it was legal to employ me yet, so at three minutes to nine the head teacher rang to find out while I went to let the class in. By the time I'd settled them on to the carpet, she came in to tell me I could be officially employed and gave me a bundle of resources. I handed over my house keys to the first familiar parent who came through the door, with instructions for her to take the dog back home, and once I'd got over the shock I really enjoyed myself.

Now the first day's over I feel much more positive about the whole idea of supply teaching.

However, it did mean that by this evening we were still no further on with the toga. I couldn't see what was wrong with a bed-sheet held up by a safety-pin but it took half an hour of careful arranging in front of a mirror to convince Emma.

I make that just the seven extra vocations this week: designer, dressmaker, nurse, diplomat, teacher, not forgetting the usual housekeeper and chef. I'm ready for the weekend now, please.

Saturday, 25 October

The start of half-term and a day out today. Emma had been given the opportunity to play her violin in a music workshop for children in one of the city centre concert halls. This would occupy her for two hours. David and Matthew headed round the corner to the science museum for two hours and I explored an interesting exhibition which was conveniently close by. We all met up back at the concert hall at the end of the workshop for a twenty-minute performance given by the hundred children who took part. For an original composition put together in so brief a time it was very impressive, with surroundings to match.

After the concert we went on together to yet another exhibition. This one was called 'Dialogue in the Dark': a forty-minute guided tour through a landscape that wasn't just dark, it was totally dark.

It wasn't just an exercise in sight deprivation: we were supposed to become more aware of our other senses. It sounded 'jolly good fun' in the publicity. In fact, it was a salutary and somewhat scary experience.

We went round in a small group with a partially sighted volunteer as our guide. He handed us our white sticks and asked us would we mind not tapping them like they do in the movies because he was doing this tour all day and the sound of eight anxious adults nervously tapping their way round the exhibition was giving him a headache. He showed us the correct way to use the sticks and we were off, with only the sound of his voice to follow. Our task was to find our way through a garden, across a road (complete with traffic noise), up an incline, into and all around a house and finally to take ourselves into a pub for a drink.

Two things struck me (well, three, actually, if you count the bush I collided with in the garden). The first was the importance of speech: we called out our names at regular intervals to help everyone stay together. The second was the importance of boundaries: for the entire forty-minute walk in the dark, I clung to any wall, fence or boundary I could find.

Our guide had the advantage over us; our forty-minute endurance test was his everyday reality. He was annoyingly calm and acutely sensitive to the tone of our voices. I was trying so hard not to sound as alarmed as I felt, but he picked up the slightest nuance of anxiety. As he patiently shepherded us around obstacles, following his voice became an exercise of trust.

I came out with a headache because I'd stared so hard into the pitch dark, trying desperately to make out any chink of light for guidance, and the whole experience seemed somehow symbolic of the year we've had. I've had a spiritual headache for most of the last six months due to spending too long on the pointless exercise of staring hard into the future wondering what it would bring. I'm glad now that I didn't know in advance what a complicated journey this year would be. At times it has felt like a long walk in the dark and I have longed to see round corners. But looking back I can now see that we were never left without the guide of God's Word or the reassurance of his voice.

I only hope my 'following technique' has been improved.

Tuesday, 28 October

Another weird dream last night: I was in a car park being chased by a big brown bear. He wasn't very friendly. I had to hide in the boot of a car. Can't think what to blame for this dream – perhaps it's my hormones. If it was meant to tell me anything I'm not sure what. Be wary of bears? Or car parks? Or combinations of the two?

Wednesday, 29 October

The builders are getting on well. They had a slight hiccup last week when they couldn't find the right bricks. Now we've got that sorted, they are making progress once again. The weather's been amazing and that's helped a lot. So far there is no sign of the winter the locals have been warning us about for weeks.

Round here they don't ask you how many years you've lived here but how many winters you've survived. Mention winter weather and everyone has a story to tell: 'blocked in for over a week', 'three-foot drifts in half an hour' and 'being stuck indoors for days' are typical. In order to understand their preoccupation you need to know that every road into our village carries bright red snow warning signs which say, 'STOP! When lights flash, road closed'.

Personally, I think the locals rather relish the dash of excitement this fact adds to an otherwise grey and wet winter experience. This suspicion was confirmed last night when one member of our house group gave us his version of the ritual winter warning and boasted about 'eight foot of snow *in* me garage wi' thi door shut'.

This particular weather conversation was one of several interesting side-tracks permitted by our house group leader during our study of Psalm 62. As usual we are discovering that it's what people say before the study, after the study and whenever we get off the subject during the study that's really interesting. This particular side-track did at least lead us back to Scripture; we got on to that verse: 'though your sins be as scarlet, they shall be like snow' and this prompted one well-informed member to tell us about the difficulties of translating that verse for tribes in Africa who've never seen snow. Apparently in their version it reads, 'your sins . . . will be like the inside of a coconut'. The same verse also gave problems for the translators for the Inuits of Greenland (amazing, what you can find out in house group!) who have an incredible fifty words for our one word 'snow' so it's rather important you find the right one: it wouldn't do to compare forgiven sins to 'the slushy stuff left over three days after a fall'.

Duly impressed by this display of linguistic insight, we all thought for a moment about what type of weather we British would excel at describing. With one voice, we concurred: rain!

Thankfully we've had very little of it lately and

the builders are on schedule; we may yet be in our own place for Christmas. Then we might have some winter tales of our own to tell.

Friday, 31 October

It's been a week full of chores. Shopping, ironing, cleaning, cooking and more shopping. I probably haven't done these things any more frequently than usual but the lack of anything interesting to do makes it feel that way.

The one inspiring element in all this has been a book I've been reading which is a series of reflections on encounters with Jesus in the gospels. Yesterday evening in bed I read about Jesus and the woman at the well. How he offered her a spring of living water that would never dry up. There's something about a bubbling spring that is the exact opposite of stale drudgery, something joyful and refreshing that is the opposite of fear or anxiety. The chapter closed with a meditation on the woman's request: 'Sir, give me this water that I may never be thirsty.'

I turned out the light and rolled over to sleep. This morning I woke with the memory of a dream. At last one worth recording. I dreamt about my dad, who died ten years ago. The whole dream was no more than a moment, a tiny clip from memory, but I saw his face so clearly and heard his laugh. We were messing about in a garden and I drenched his face with the spray from a garden hose. It was a joyful kind of dream, an easy kind of familiarity.

Now I've written it down I'm not going to analyse it for layers of meaning. I'd far rather savour the flavours of joy and completeness that came with it.

Sunday, 2 November

What a dull weekend. The weather has been a big disappointment even if the company's been great. My close friend Ruth came up on the train on Friday with her two children. I've been telling her for months what a beautiful place we live in and when she finally comes up the clouds come down, obscuring all the hills.

At least we were able to show her over the house. Three weeks of work completed in glorious sunshine, 'the sunniest autumn for forty years' I heard on the radio the other day; what an answer to prayer. Even if the weather breaks now most of the external stuff is done and the builders are estimating three more weeks to complete the job.

It was great to show Ruth our new home as she was the one who has followed the whole process from the very beginning. Before she left this afternoon we attempted to pray together. I use the word 'attempted' because with four children under the age of nine in the house, peace and quiet was at a premium.

We'd just got past the 'thank you for a lovely weekend together' bit and were about to get to the nitty-gritty of the week ahead when I had to break off because the word 'FEEHART' had been shoved under my nose. The children were playing a spelling game on the computer and had got stuck.

'It's all muddled up. We don't know what it is,' they complained.

We had to put the Lord on hold for two minutes while we worked out the anagram.

Maybe I'm a poor disciplinarian, maybe my children should have been more respectful of parents engaged in such serious spiritual pursuits, but then again I feel that if I've been given permission to burst urgently into God's presence with whatever need occurs to me (something I frequently do), I have to allow my children similar access to me. They had at least loitered for half a minute before disturbing us.

Interrupted prayer must be a standard feature of life for any Christian parent. The tricky bit is to offer our offspring the same welcome, the same listening ear that we ourselves are receiving from God. How often have I broken off a prayer time with an impatient, 'Oh, *what* is it now?' only to sense a divine raising of the eyebrow. 'Suffer the little children', what an apt phrase!

(The word was 'feather'.)

Monday, 3 November

I was up and dressed by seven thirty this morning. David was very surprised. I don't usually feature in his morning routine. For someone who normally wakes at twenty to eight (and only then if a cup of tea is deposited on her bedside table) and gets out of bed by eight on a good day, this new routine may become a bit of a strain.

The reason for this sudden onset of early rising is the fact that I am now on the local authority's list of supply teachers, so I could be offered a day's work at a moment's notice. This sounds all very exciting, as if I've joined a sort of flying squad stand-in for teachers. The reality is rather different: dressed, ready to teach, sandwiches packed and pencils sharpened, I waited and waited . . . nothing happened. By twenty to nine I realised nothing would and reckoned the day was my own again so I planned accordingly. But I can't make plans for tomorrow, of course, because tomorrow I may be at work. A 'control freak' like me is going to have a hard time with such an unpredictable schedule. I like to sit down at the end of each day and write my list of chores for the following day. I find it difficult

'I could be offered a day's work at a moment's notice'

to keep space in my mind, let alone on my list, for sudden rescheduling.

Tuesday, 4 November

As I sat by my silent phone this morning I was reminded of the wise and foolish virgins waiting for the bridegroom and I felt a lot of sympathy for the foolish ones. Being in a constant state of readiness is a very exhausting business. It's only Day 2 of the new routine and I was struggling to get out of bed this morning. But I must persevere; I have a feeling that the first morning I snatch an extra ten minutes in bed will be the first morning I'm offered work and then chaos will break out in all directions. The thought of trying to get two children and one adult, three lunch boxes and an assorted set of resources, spelling lists and reading books, all delivered to different educational institutes by five to nine in the morning strikes me as a logistical nightmare possibly not worth a day's pay. But that's defeatist talk. I must stay positive and keep setting the alarm.

The parable of the bridegroom reminds me of the ultimate reason for readiness. I saw a poster once that said: 'Jesus is coming back' in large letters and added underneath, in a smaller font, '. . . maybe today'. What a radical difference it would make to my lists and my expectations if I always kept that possibility in mind.

Wednesday, 5 November

Hooray, today I had work. Even better, they didn't phone me this morning, they phoned me yesterday lunchtime. So I had the luxury of a whole afternoon spent preparing good lessons only to turn up this morning to find the teacher had left some work anyway. Oh well, such is life.

After tea we went up to look at the house again and found progress has been depressingly slow. We couldn't really see any difference from last weekend but they must have been doing something for the last three days. I suppose once the major brickwork is finished the smaller things don't seem so obvious. We went round listing all the things that we would need to do once the builders are finished. The list was overwhelmingly long. David's pay is for the mortgage, mine is for the carpets, furnishings, etc. And the two days' pay I've so far earned is not going to get us very far down the list. I came home and fretted about how on earth we were going to afford it all. I worried instead of praying because I have a hard time praying about money at the best of times. I know my heavenly Father knows what I need, but does he know what I like?

It also seems so unspiritual to be preoccupied with carpets and curtains when there are so many starving children in the world. It didn't help when I turned up my Bible reading for today and read the story of the rich young ruler who was told to give up everything he had. This is not the kind of story I want to hear just when I've written a long list of all the things I want to buy. But perhaps it is the story I need to hear: money is nothing, neither good nor bad; it can get in the way or it can be put to good use. However much or however little we have doesn't matter; what matters is that it doesn't become the be all and end all of our lives.

In the end I told David I was worrying about money and he prayed about it for me and told me not to fret. I'll take that as an order.

Saturday, 8 November

It's rained heavily for the last two days and the roof of our extension has no tiles. The builder doesn't seem to be worried about this but it makes me uneasy to have half my house open to the elements, especially when the elements are so inclement.

We didn't get much done up at the house today because it was a church work day and David spent the morning painting pipes down in the boiler room. In the afternoon we went to a fortieth birthday party. The fact that we still have five years to go before we are forty was not the only reason we enjoyed it. Many of our friends were there and an entertaining conversation ambled around 'the Saturday experience of family life': buying shoes, choosing wallpaper, ferrying children to parties and so on.

One friend told us he'd started the day at 5.00 a.m. having been rudely woken by a synthesised voice telling him to: 'Eat laser light, Punk! Eat laser light, Punk! Eat laser light, Punk!'

Tracing this phenomenon to his son's bedroom he eventually located a malfunctioning (and none too friendly) toy emitting these futile threats from the depths of a toy box. Needless to say, Son had slept on unawares while Dad made his dawn raid and extracted the batteries.

Such are the hazards of High-Tech Parenthood. We don't allow batteries in our house – at least we wouldn't if I had anything to do with it. As it is, Emma's cyberpet runs on batteries and bleeps incessantly and, not to be outdone, Matthew has a key fob that plays one bar of a heavy metal 'tune' (I use the word advisedly) at the press of a button. Naturally if you keep your finger on the button it plays two, three, four, five bars of the same 'tune', over and over and over.

At such moments the limited life-span of a battery seems a blessing. I only hope no one invents a longer-lasting energy source without warning parents first. Sources of energy in toys are one thing, sources of energy for kids are quite another. My two seem to function pretty well on peanut butter sandwiches, chocolate Weetos and nine hours' sleep a night.

Lately, however, Matthew has been concerned that he's not getting enough sleep and has become obsessed with getting to bed early. Last night he was in his pyjamas for half six, when his light doesn't normally go out till half seven. I know it is illogical to worry about a sudden onset of good behaviour but that's parenthood for you. I shall feel better when he returns to his normal 'any excuse to stay up' routine.

My own limited store of energy has frustrated me this week. When I feel my own batteries are running down, I feel defeated. But tonight, as I tucked Matthew into bed (in time for a full twelve hours) it occurred to me that all the best words come after reaching that point of complete exhaustion: rest, relax, replenish, revive, refuel, reinvigorate . . . (and I'm sure there must be some that don't begin with 'r').

A quiet cup of tea, twenty minutes with a book, a long soak in the bath, a walk with the dog, life would be so dull without such restorative pleasures. Perhaps I'm glad I don't have long-life batteries after all.

Sunday, 9 November

Remembrance Sunday, and I woke up feeling restless and inadequate. Ever since we were transplanted here last June, I've suffered from a sense of purposelessness. Many of the roles I had that gave my life meaning were wrenched away from me. I've enjoyed the rest but now I feel ready to be a part of something again. I don't just want to be a pew-filler, I want to be involved. I don't just want to say something, anything, to anyone to pass the time of day, I want to have something to say, something that makes a difference. I'm probably running ahead of myself. Until the house is straight and we are settled in, I can't see me being able to take on anything else.

Tuesday, 11 November

Poor David. I snarled at him this morning before he left for work simply because he'd asked me what was my plan for the day. He was only showing an interest, but it felt as if I was being held accountable and my sense of inadequacy has lingered since Sunday. I feel a failure for every morning when I am not offered work. I know this is illogical and I wouldn't want to work every day anyway, but I still feel let down when the phone doesn't ring.

Thursday, 13 November

Had half a day's work yesterday. Still doing calculations on the back of envelopes but managing not to worry as much as I did last week. Looking forward to Saturday's 'Vocations Day'; perhaps this will help sort out my lack of purpose.

Saturday, 15 November

True to form for an Anglican event, I turned up this morning for the Vocations Day knowing only where it would be held and how long it would last, and this second item of information proved to be incorrect. I had been given the general idea that it would be a day to explore the varying vocations for ministry within the Church of England but I had no idea who would be there to lead it, so it was a surprise on arrival to find out that at least a hundred other people had also turned up on the basis of the few published facts.

The whole day exceeded both my expectations and its own publicity. We were divided into groups and given half-hour slots with about eight different specialists. There were a Church Army officer, a nun, a paid priest, an unpaid priest, several Readers and some ladies to talk about lay ministry.

The nun was the most interesting. I haven't met that many nuns so I was really intrigued to meet a woman my age who had followed that calling. She spoke about her lifestyle, her service, how her family felt about her calling, the rigours of community life and so on. All very interesting, but I couldn't take my eyes off her shoes. I may be a low-minded materialist, but they looked the comfiest pair of mules I'd ever seen, so when she took questions at the end I asked her where she'd bought them. (I did at least wait till all the 'spiritual' questions from the rest of my group had dried up.) She told me they were from Covent Garden and very expensive. 'So how come you're wearing them?' was on the tip of my tongue but I just managed not to be so rude. I like the idea of a nun wearing expensive shoes. Clearly poverty ain't what it used to be.

At the end of the day I came away confirmed in my original choice to continue with my Readership training. None of the other options rang bells with me. I think being a Reader allows me to serve in the way I feel gifted. This was quite a relief because most of the other vocations are not readily accessible to working mothers with homes and families to run.

I came back to find David painting and the children playing. There had been real progress at last: a hole knocked through downstairs, my dishwasher plumbed in and my cooker installed. It was great to see these two essential kitchen elements in place even if I won't be using them for a few weeks yet. The builders had been there for most of the day and told David that they couldn't do any more until the plasterers did their stuff on Monday.

Tuesday, 18 November

This is the sixth week of building work, the final week . . . allegedly. The plasterers were meant to turn up yesterday and didn't. No sign of them again this morning. Sub-contractors seem to run to their own timetable.

Wednesday, 19 November

No plasterers again today. No work done on the house and no work for me. I know I ought to trust that God knows what I can and what I can't handle, but it still feels like a waking-up to a rejection every morning when I don't get offered work. I couldn't have handled work today anyway: not only am I pre-menstrual, I'm too preoccupied with the house. Last night's home group was a study on Psalm 142, a psalm of desperation. It seemed somehow appropriate.

Thursday, 20 November

The good news today was that the plasterers arrived. The bad news is that they took one look at the place and said they couldn't do their stuff until the plumber had finished his, and off they went.

Friday, 21 November

The plumber came yesterday and fiddled with a bit here and a bit there. Today he went off sick. The plasterers returned only to tell me they still couldn't work if the electrician was still there, which he was. They went away again. They don't seem very keen to work, these plasterers, certainly not as part of a team. We are not impressed.

Now that most of this week has been wasted we are a week behind in time. Yesterday evening I had a carpet salesman round to measure up for bedroom carpets. He had to walk up a plank to get into the house and find his way round with a torch (no light sockets in new rooms yet). He couldn't believe that I was actually asking him to measure up for carpets in unplastered rooms, with holes in the floor and no skirting boards. I had to admit the prospect of the place being ready on time did seem far-fetched, but carpets take time to order and we were hoping to have them down before we move in, hopefully in two weeks' time.

If we do have carpets down it will be a bonus. I was also hoping to have time to clean through and wash curtains beforehand, but at the rate we are going it's beginning to look as if we'll have to move in with the builders still there.

It's rained every day for the last three weeks and this hasn't helped. The house is presently surrounded by its own mud-filled moat which is forded at the entrances by slippery planks of wood. The existing carpets in the house are caked in mud and we may not be able to salvage them (more expense).

All this and Christmas too! My list of things to do runs to four sides of A4.

Saturday, 22 November

At least this morning I made progress with Christmas. A friend took me to a craft fair and in one hour of decisive shopping I bought almost all the presents for the wider family. I impressed myself with my efficiency, but I simply didn't have time to dither.

Last night I told David that the needle on my personal stress-level indicator was hovering near the maximum mark, 'One more setback and I'll be a quivering heap of hysteria,' were my precise words. So what happened this morning while I was out shopping? The fridge in our new kitchen burst into flames and died. Thankfully this happened while David was there; if it had happened on any of the many days when the house has stood empty we might not have had a house to move into. The fact that we had narrowly avoided this greater disaster made the smaller one easier to cope with. But then this afternoon, while they were plumbing in the central heating system, the builders routed the water through the dining-room ceiling (the perfectly decent 'didn't used to need decorating' dining-room ceiling).

I thought water was meant to go through pipes, myself.

I feel the quivers coming on, I'm on my way to lie down. If someone would just wake me up when it's all over.

Sunday, 23 November

Woke up feeling low with a capital 'L'. The cold that started yesterday in my throat has reached my nose and Emma seems to have caught it as well. The one good thing about today was an invite to supper with some friends who didn't mind germs. Not having to cook was a real help.

Monday, 24 November

Spent today wrapping Christmas presents and sniffing. Emma spent the day at home as well although her cold doesn't seem too bad. I have decided that if I can't get on with the house, then at least I can get through all the Christmas chores. I was just getting into this activity when I was offered a day's work tomorrow, which cheered me somewhat.

Tuesday, 25 November

Woke at five thirty and went and sat on the bathroom floor, the only place I can go that won't disturb the children or the dog. I knew I wouldn't get back to sleep so there didn't seem much point staying in bed, but I hate sitting in cold, early-morning bathrooms. I tried to read but all I did was fret: stress, stress, stress, money, money, money, mess, mess, mess, work, work, work . . . it all went round and round in my head. It can be very disorientating when you don't know which bit of your life to worry about most. I did at least pray and that seemed to help. I also read Psalm 63 where David writes, 'On my bed I remember you; I think of you through the watches of the night.' I know how he feels, only I don't expect he ever sat on a bathroom floor.

The day in school went well, so that's something.

Wednesday, 26 November

Spent the day writing Christmas cards and sniffing for real. This time it was emotion, not cold. It was really hard to be writing cards to people from our old church who we would have greeted in person last year. It made our presence here seem so final somehow. Into all this gloom shone at least one verse that I came across in the morning: 'Let him who walks in the dark, who has no light, trust in the name of the LORD and rely on his God' (Isaiah 50:10).

Thursday, 27 November

At last some progress on the house. The plasterers

have come and done their stuff this week. The picture is no longer looking quite so dismal; we may still be able to move in just over a week's time. A little candle of hope has been lit: the boiler is working, the fire is in, the place is warming up.

Saturday, 29 November

So little time, so much to do, so little dosh! At least today we had our first full Saturday together in the house and we made good progress. One week from today and we hope to be in. Now that moving is really beginning to look likely I have allowed myself to get excited. The hassles of the last few weeks have fallen away. I can see the end result and it will all be worth it. The time-table for the next week is still quite tight but we think it can be done. At least I've cracked Christmas this last week. The cards are all written and all the presents purchased and wrapped up to keep them from prying eyes in the move. My cold has abated and so has Emma's, and I hope the Slough of Despond is behind us.

Monday, 1 December

Couldn't get to sleep last night. Lay awake from half eleven till half one. For the first time in a long time it wasn't anxiety that was keeping me awake, it was excitement. This time next week the move will be over, the children will go back to school and I shall have a whole day on my own in my *own* house. I can't wait. Living in a rented house has made me realise how territorial I am. Owning my own space seems so important somehow. I don't know why I've found having a landlady so hard, it's not as if I've ever wanted to spread jam on the carpet or draw on the walls and it hasn't been that much of a strain keeping this place clean, but my heart hasn't been in it. I guess it's just hard to home-make when it isn't your home.

So at last I'm allowing myself to get excited about being in our own place. I was arranging my furnishings in my head for half the night, wondering if the sofa will fit in the space we have planned for it, how my desk will look in the study and whether the curtains from the hall would look better in the spare room. Other people, more organised than us, sit down and draw scale plans before they extend their house. They draw all their furniture to scale on squared paper, then place it on a scaled-down room also drawn out on squared paper. They lie awake at night and calculate how many sockets they are going to need; they plan everything down to the final centimetre before they so much as lift a trowel. I know such people exist, I've met at least two of them. But we're not like that. When the architect came round we said, 'Please can we have a room from about here to about here, and another room on top, two double sockets in each and the usual number of doors and windows.'

Considering we were so unspecific, things have turned out rather well. Our bedroom is much bigger than we'd expected it to be, which will be a real treat, and even the spare room isn't small. All the bedrooms we've ever shared up to now have had a stingy two-foot space on three sides round the bed. In our new room the bed will be at least eight feet from the door!

All my excitement was still tinged slightly at the edges with anxiety. 'What if the house burns down before we move in?' (no reason why it should, but 'what if' all the same), 'What if the builders don't finish in time?', 'What if the roof caves in?', 'What if five hungry bears come out of the woods and eat us all up?' The more tired I became the more irrational my fears. Eventually I crossed the barrier into sleep and had dreadful dreams all night: sudden deaths, head-on collisions, earthquakes, tornados – you name it, I dreamt it. My subconscious was clearly having a hard time relaxing back into the fact that we would move next Saturday and all would be well.

My subconscious was right. Today was a disaster. When I arrived at the house I found that instead of the expected team of five familiar workmen to finish the job, I'd been sent one short, strange one. I'd never met Scrumpy before, and to say I wasn't impressed would be an understatement. He wasn't much over five foot, had a black eye, an unsteady gait and spent the whole ten minutes I was there hunting for a blow torch to light his first fag of the working day. When I went back later he nonchalantly told me he'd gone round to a neighbour's to ask for a match and she'd given him the whole box. I'm not surprised, she was probably terrified.

The second thing that went wrong was that our landlady dropped in to say that she thought we owed her more money than the agent said we did (with a budget as finely balanced as ours this was seriously bad news). I managed to disagree as politely as I could but felt seriously stressed. When she'd gone I packed with renewed vigour; I can't wait to get out of here.

I heard the final piece of bad news on the radio: the weather forecast for Saturday is snow.

By the time David came in from work I was nearing hysteria. Scrumpy had completed the one task he'd been sent to do: finish a drain. He'd no sooner finished it when the building inspector came along and failed it. The place is still a long way from the word 'inhabitable', and we're supposed to move in next Saturday. I just don't know how we're going to do this.

Tuesday, 2 December

Thank you, thank you, thank you, thank you! Home group this evening was on gratitude and I *am* deeply grateful. Everything that went wrong yesterday turned out right today. The proper builders returned and put the drain right just before the building inspector returned and passed it. The agent sided with us over how much we owe the landlady, and even the long-range weather forecast has improved.

The builders promised tomorrow would be their last day. I hope they're right.

Friday, 5 December

The builders left yesterday, only one day later than promised. That gave us today to ourselves in the house to clean. David had the day off, and we started with some good news, then some bad news. The spare part for the fridge came in the post. That was the good news. David fitted it and the fridge sprang into life for about thirty seconds before a second small component fizzed and died. That was the bad news. For several moments I was sorely tempted to give up on the whole heap of junk and go out and spend several hundred pounds we haven't got on a new one.

'I never liked that fridge. Anyway, it's too big for this kitchen.'

David pointed out that, in spite of my aesthetic preferences, our extreme lack of funds meant that £2.50 plus postage and packing for a second small part would be the sensible option. I hate sensible options.

Even so, I got on the phone and persuaded the electrical component people to put a spare part in the post NOW instead of waiting for our cheque to arrive and clear like they did last time.

David continued with the heavy-duty cleaning all afternoon while I went shopping. I didn't want to go shopping. I thought buying a load of food that would need refrigerating demonstrated a foolhardy faith in electrical component companies and the GPO. But I went anyway. David would not move house on an empty stomach and it was best to humour him.

By teatime I was agitating to be in our own house.

'Go then, why don't you? There's nothing stopping you sleeping there tonight if you want to,' David suggested.

'Okay then, I will,' I declared (having first checked that Emma would come with me; I didn't fancy it on my own).

So here we are, tucked into two sleeping-bags on the floor in what will be Matthew's bedroom. What we lack in furnishing we make up for in warmth. We brought up our bubble bath and skin creams and treated ourselves to a two long, hot soaks in our very own Jacuzzi bath! Emma wasn't too sure about the Jacuzzi bit but once I'd turned on the bubbles she was quickly convinced. I left her wallowing while I pottered downstairs.

It suddenly dawned on me that buying a house with a Jacuzzi bath is an amazing piece of serendipity. Almost two years ago, when our whole moving house saga started, we wanted to buy a house with a Jacuzzi bath. We didn't want it just for the bath, it just happened to have one (and also four bedrooms, a study and an Aga). I was heartbroken when someone else bought that house. Now, two years later and three hundred miles away, I finally get a Jacuzzi bath! (Not to mention four bedrooms and a study.) I hadn't thought of it before, but it suddenly seemed that God had planned out even the seemingly superfluous details. I felt very loved.

I went upstairs to remind Emma of this story but, not for the first time, I found her thoughts had gone in the same direction. Before I said anything she asked me if I remembered that house we had tried to buy. She was equally impressed with God's attention to detail. I don't think we specified a Jacuzzi when we prayed for the right house!

One other lovely thing happened today: a tiny cutting came carefully wrapped up through the post. It smelt exquisite. I was astonished: first that such a tiny plant could have such a stunning fragrance and, second, that such a fragile thing could tolerate being uprooted, wrapped up in a box and parcelled off to a new destination.

The friend who had sent it had lovingly cultivated it from a cutting taken from the shores of Lake Galilee. She sent it to us as a metaphor of our being uprooted and parcelled off 'up north'. It was accompanied by a prayer that we would soon start to feel 'rooted'.

Immediately I rushed out to the shed and potted up my precious plant. (I have a house, now I have a house plant!) It seems to somehow express my own life, so I am willing it not to wilt. It's already stretching new shoots skyward on my kitchen windowsill and spreading its fragrance into the kitchen: the scent of survival.

Monday, 8 December

The long-awaited Monday has arrived! The weekend move went very well thanks to eight sturdy friends who lifted and carried, one hired van and one other good friend who took the children out of the way for the whole of Saturday. The snow didn't materialise – it didn't even rain. The fridge part came in the post and the fridge now works, my kitchen cupboards are full, half my boxes are unpacked, the kitchen is straight and after month

'Eight sturdy friends who lifted and carried'

of feeling out of context, I am at last able to own my surroundings. I am almost in my right mind.

This is a hundred per cent improvement in our circumstances and I am deeply grateful. It was a joy to walk the children to school this morning, walk home to my own home and shut my own front door behind me knowing I had six hours to happily potter among my own things. (Repetition of the word 'own' is entirely deliberate.)

Only the dog is unhappy. He doesn't like being shut downstairs in the kitchen at night instead of sleeping outside our bedroom door. He registered his misery at five this morning by scratching on the kitchen door. I was not best pleased; he woke me up and I couldn't get back to sleep. I hope he gets used to his new surroundings soon.

Tuesday, 9 December

It's been like Christmas come early, unpacking all those boxes that were packed up in June and finding so many things we'd forgotten about, gifts we'd been given, favourite books, photo albums. Today I've concentrated on the study and had a very happy time arranging all my books on the shelves. I spent a long time fiddling around with the desk and the filing cabinets, trying to work out what would fit. In the end the old computer desk wouldn't fit. The computer could go on my main desk but what to do with the old desk? I took it up to the spare room and discovered it would make an ideal sewing table. Pulling it into place and plonking my sewing machine on top, I realised there was even a socket just where I needed it. Brilliant! Who needs forward planning? Meanwhile, downstairs, getting rid of the desk left room for a chair. What more could I want? A desk, two filing cabinets, loads of shelves and a thinking chair: my joy was complete.

I picked up my Bible this evening and read a portion in 1 Peter about being 'strangers'. A sentence in the Bible notes caught my eye: 'We should feel a little as if we do not belong, that we are only passing through.' Great. Just as I'm settling in I'm reminded that no home is permanent. God said the very same thing to me eighteen months ago when we first considered moving here. It sounds as if I'm not meant to forget it.

Thursday, 11 December

David went back to work yesterday and life is returning to normality, except that I don't yet know what form normality will take up here. I can't believe that I've been in the longed-for house for less than a week and already the anti-climax has set in. Last night's dream didn't help. I dreamt about Dad again. This time I dreamt that he hadn't died, he'd just left home without any explanation, and years later I found him but he still wouldn't say why he left. It was a very disturbing dream. When I woke up I had to spend several minutes reminding myself that he had in fact died and that it wasn't his fault. Even so, the sense of abandonment lingered and coloured my day. It's great having a new house but dreadful having no one to show it to. That's not quite true: there are lots of local new friends I can share it with, but as yet no one who really counts, no one like Dad.

I hauled myself back to 'normality' in the afternoon by going along to the school Christmas Carol Concert. It was excellently done and reassuringly biblical.

Saturday, 13 December

Yesterday I failed to buy a lounge carpet. I spent two hours in a carpet shop clutching a sofa cushion and still failed. I'd taken the sofa cushion to match up the colours but discovered our sofa is a very unmatchable green. The poor salesman disassembled most of his stock in a bid to find something I liked, all for nothing. I was about to settle on something when it occurred to me I needed to pay for this carpet with a credit card.

'Do you take credit cards?' (I admit it was rather stupid to ask this at the end of the process, not the beginning.) Unfortunately, he didn't.

So today, once again armed with part of the sofa and a credit card, we went to look at four more carpet shops. We failed again and ended up in a DIY store by the late afternoon, where I had an idea.

'What about a rug?'

'What about a rug?'

'In the lounge, what about a rug in the lounge?'

David went pale. We went to find the fact sheets on sanding, staining and varnishing floors and didn't reach a decision. It isn't urgent to do the lounge anyway; maybe we should just shut the door on it until the January sales.

Sunday, 14 December

Yesterday there wasn't any urgency about decorating the lounge. There is now. All the family and half a dozen friends have decided to come and see us before, during and after Christmas.

'We'd love to see your new house, we won't mind the mess.'

Yes, but you haven't seen the mess and you just can't celebrate Christmas in a lounge that looks like a concrete bunker. So now we have a deadline to finish the lounge and I have a large group of people who count to show round my house, which is very gratifying. The first set arrive next Sunday so we have a heavy week's decorating ahead of us.

Monday, 15 December

I went and bought the rug today and found a very helpful assistant who calculated the surface area of my lounge floor and told me how many tins of wood stain and varnish I'd need. The rug is black, which matches the TV, the fire and curtain rails but not the sofa, thankfully. It's meant to contrast with the sofa.

I hired an industrial sander for Wednesday and made a start on the ceiling. Diluted white emulsion gets everywhere. My face is a mass of white spots and my hair has gone grey.

When David got home the ceiling was finished and my head was locked back at a forty-five-degree angle to the rest of my body. A long soak in the bath and I straightened out.

Wednesday, 17 December

I was painting by half past six again this morning. I got the first coat of paint on the walls yesterday and half the second coat on yesterday evening. I needed to finish the second coat early on in the day so it would dry before I brought the sander home and sent sawdust everywhere.

This enthusiasm for home improvements seems to be contagious. I have found a neighbour keen to sand her bedroom floor so we've gone halves with the sander, which has saved us both a bit. I agreed to collect it this lunchtime but I didn't come straight home with it. Instead I wandered into a curtain shop and came out forty minutes later, £180 worse off and with yards and yards of fabric in my arms. I don't know quite how it happened. I fully intended to buy ready-made curtains, but the very persuasive shopkeeper convinced me otherwise. I told her all the colours I had in the room so far and she came up with a beautiful fabric: black Latin words on a honey-coloured background. My Latin isn't great but I could at least make out the words 'Glory to God' and 'faith', which sounded good to me. I hope the rest of the text is as sound. (David offered his translation when I showed him the fabric this evening: 'Guess how much these curtains cost me.')

I'm trying not to think about the fact that I've never made lined curtains in my life before; the lady in the shop said it was easy and cut all the lengths for me, which was more than kind. Anyway, making curtains is Friday's job.

Today's job was nearly scuppered before it began. Having lugged the sander into the house I couldn't get it to start. After five minutes' frustrated fiddling, I called the hire shop. Twenty minutes later assistance arrived. Of course, it worked for him. Why wouldn't it work for me? I have no idea, but at least it carried on working after he was gone.

Thursday, 18 December

I stood in the post office queue this morning and worried. I had plenty of time to worry; it was a long queue. I was worrying about Christmas: how on earth was I going to cater for several groups of ten guests at a time with only a kitchen table that sat four? Buying a decent size dining-room table was on the list, but a long way down. I worried my way to the front of the queue and when I got there a little voice in my head said, 'Tell Enid about your problem.' I couldn't see how telling the post office lady would help but for once I was obedient. Her response was astonishing.

'We have a spare table and chairs we're not using. Would you like to borrow them?'

I raced hurriedly through the 'well, no, I couldn't possibly', 'are you sure?' and 'if it wouldn't be any trouble' and landed quickly at 'yes, please, that would be wonderful'.

I skipped home.

Friday, 19 December

Curtain day. Thankfully I found a book yesterday with a set of 'how to make curtains' instructions complete with diagrams. It looked easy, but wrestling twenty-five yards of fabric through a sewing machine in the hope that some acceptable window-dressing will result was never going to be easy. It took all day just to sew them and two hours this evening to iron them. But they are almost finished. I'll hang them tomorrow.

Saturday, 20 December

This morning was a real celebration; we took the kids to do their Christmas shopping and came home with bags of secrets, sticky buns for lunch and a real Christmas tree. The tree had been an impulse buy. I couldn't face sticking our scrawny old plastic one into our newly decorated room. At lunchtime we collected the loaned table and six chairs. We added our old kitchen table on the end, threw a cloth over and, hey presto, seating for ten.

I went out again in the afternoon and when I came back David and the children had hauled the new rug into place. It fitted widthways (just) and was also much longer than I'd expected (so much for all that sanding, staining and varnishing, most of it was now under the carpet!) but it looked great.

Matthew said grace for us as we sat down to tea. He thanked God for a long list of items including the Christmas tree, loaned table, new rug and new curtains, before concluding with the words 'with love from the Bridge family. Amen'.

There is a real sense of God's pleasure in our pleasure. After so long spent wondering, waiting and worrying, it's wonderful to finally be here and feel that we've arrived. Our first visitors arrive tomorrow.

Tuesday, 23 December

Two sets of visitors down and two sets to go. The second group left today and now we are on our own till Saturday.

Boxing Day

We were sitting watching television about six o'clock on Christmas Eve when there was an almighty crash.

'What was that?' we cried in unison. Peering out into the inky blackness we saw parts of our house being blown across the patio. This was somewhat alarming. By the time David and I got out there chunks of plastic cladding were littered all over our lawn and there were the beginnings of a hole in the side of the house. Sheets of roofing felt flapped in the wind.

It was incredibly windy. How had I not noticed this from inside? I'd been baking and cooking and preparing all day and hadn't given much thought to the weather – well, you don't, do you, until it blows parts of your house away.

David was all for going up a ladder and banging

a few planks over the hole and securing the flapping felt. In a scene vaguely reminiscent of some black-and-white melodrama I pleaded with him not to. He got as far as putting the ladder against the wall when a gust of wind almost blew me off my feet, and the two frightened faces looking out from inside persuaded him to put away the ladder.

The damage wasn't too bad; so long as no more came off we would survive the night. The children were a bit shaken and went off to bed, one of them wondering if the chimney Santa was meant to climb down would still be there for him by the time he arrived and the other wondering if the TV aerial would survive the night.

David and I spent a very restless night listening to the wind rattle the tiles and tear at the loose felt. I confess the first thing I did on Christmas morning was run down and check the TV still worked. It did. What a relief; I didn't feel up to an old-fashioned Christmas with no TV.

After the presents were opened David spent an hour up the ladder before church. The hole had got worse; we were down to one layer of brick between the bathroom and the outside. David banged up a temporary repair with offers of help from at least three neighbours we'd never met before, a nice touch of Christmas spirit.

The rest of the day passed uneventfully, apart from the fact that we were unusually diligent about listening to weather forecasts. A lot of people were worse off than us, some without power. We ate our Christmas meal thoughtfully and thankfully.

Saturday, 27 December

The weather hasn't improved. The wind has died down but the rain has been heavy and some of it has been seeping into our house. Our brand new wall appears to leak. We have damp patches in three places, which is a bit depressing.

David's family arrive today and I'm disappointed to be showing them a house with damp patches and a hole in the side. I also woke up thinking about the fact that today is the tenth anniversary of my dad's death. This is the third house I have lived in that he hasn't seen. And our house isn't the only thing that's changed over the years. The grandchildren he never met have grown older and life has become more complex somehow. Simple answers to complex questions don't seem so helpful any more.

Listen to me – three damp patches, one old sorrow and I'm moaning on like a melancholic misery. For most of the last three weeks I've been floating on air about the house and now someone's punctured my balloon. Feelings are so fickle. I turned to my daily reading this morning and was pleased to see it was Psalm 139, one of my father's favourite psalms. As

I read through the well-known phrases – 'you have searched me and you know me', 'you are familiar with all my ways', 'you have laid your hand upon me' and 'all the days ordained for me were written in your book before one of them came to be' I felt surrounded by God's presence and the peace that comes from knowing yourself understood. I may be fickle but I know I am loved.

Monday, 29 December

Gran and I went shopping today. We left the kids playing with their toys and David varnishing the doors. There are eleven unvarnished pine doors in our house. The fact that they are unvarnished doesn't bother me in the least but David is desperate to get them varnished. He tries hard not to sound as enthusiastic as he undoubtedly is, telling us that eleven doors with three coats each side means sixty-six coats of varnish 'but no, you go shopping, I can manage'.

We left him to it. He's happy really, no one's forcing him to varnish the doors.

New Year's Eve

The last group of guests, my family, will arrive by lunchtime and stay for two days. I know it will be hard when they go because I've looked forward to them coming so much. Once they are gone there will be nothing to look forward to; at least that's how it feels. Life has to settle down. We need to adapt to all the changes of the last year. I need to take my eyes off the past and fix them hopefully on the future. This won't be easy.

I know the difference between today and tomorrow is only one digit, but somehow I want to make the difference bigger this year. I need a fresh start, and I turned to the Psalms to once again put my feelings into words. Psalm 51. A psalm of repentance. I needed to repent of all the worry, all the doubt, all the resistance to God's ideas. My journey through the last twelve months has not been an easy one.

'Create in me a new heart, O God,' I prayed, for only you can create such a thing. 'Renew a right spirit within me.' I need a make-over, Lord, not a physical one but a spiritual fresh start, I need a non-fearful, non-bitter spirit. 'Do not cast me from your presence or take your Holy Spirit from me. Restore to me the joy of your salvation.' Revive my passion for eternal things and help me to think about something other than houses. 'Grant me a willing spirit to sustain me,' don't let me flag at the first defeat. 'Then I will teach transgressors your ways and sinners will turn back to you,' then maybe I'll be fruitful for you here in this new location.

Epilogue

It's now almost six months since I prayed my prayer for a new start on New Year's Eve. As I write now we have almost lived in this village for a year. I'm tempted to say it feels like a lifetime. The five years we spent in our previous location seem, by a trick of memory, to have been a 'golden era', a sunshiny time when our children were small: birthday parties, paddling pools and climbing frames.

But memory is selective and often unreliable. The only reason the past seems more attractive than the present is because the present still feels unfamiliar. Our house as yet holds no memories for us. We haven't yet claimed our own garden, let alone a place in our community.

These things take time. About three years I reckon, from arrival to starting to feel at home. Counselling is rarely offered as part of the relocation package but it ought to be considered, especially for the spouse who is simply following along in the wake of the wage-earner. It has been easier for David and the children to settle here, they have places to go and things to do. I have found it much harder. January and February were particularly bleak: I walked the children to school in the morning, collected them in the afternoon and beyond those two markers the days were a blank.

In March I got a job. With virtually no experience I became a Reception teacher for three days a week. For the first month the only good thing about the job was that it got me out of the house. The bad things were exhaustion and feeling totally out of my depth. I came very close to giving up but I knew if I did, my battered self-esteem would never recover.

What with the demands of the job my routine of prayer and Bible reading had virtually disappeared and if the truth was told I was pretty miffed with God altogether. Why had he spent so long in our last home teaching the value of friendships and community as opposed to self-reliance and independence only to then pull me out of that community?

The next thing that happened was a holiday with some old friends. It was a 'spend a lot of money' type holiday, our first ever. We had a brilliant time. My Bible lay in the bottom of my suitcase for the whole two weeks we were away and I didn't even feel guilty. The therapy of laughter and the familiarity of old friends worked wonders. I was grateful for the good time but I still wasn't speaking to God.

And then he spoke to me. Yet again it was a

dream, a recurrent theme of this past year. I dreamt I'd been asked to speak at some church event and when I had finished, I wasn't even thanked. The organisers were rushing on to some much more important event and I was overlooked. I woke up boiling over with fury and resentment, composing an indignant letter of complaint in my head. Even though I was fully awake the dream had stirred strong feelings. In the darkness of our room as David slept on beside me, the Holy Spirit spoke: 'You are angry and resentful at God. You feel unappreciated and overlooked. You feel as if God has shoved you in a corner and gone on to someone, some place more important . . .' There was a long pause during which I acknowledged that all of that was true, I was very angry and very hurt.

And then the rebuke: 'God does not owe you his appreciation, Sheila, you owe him yours.'

It might disappoint you to know that I did not fall to my knees in repentance in response to this revelation. I acknowledged it was true, was grateful for the clarification and went back to sleep. The next morning I did repent of my attitude towards God. Nothing spectacular happened, I just asked for yet another fresh start. I still didn't pick up my Bible but I did feel that somewhere deep inside I'd turned a corner. Several nights later I dreamt again. This time Jesus was praying for me, with his hands on my head. In my dream I felt an incredible sense of blessing and wholeness and I woke up with a feeling of awe.

I feel choked up as I write because I still can't tell you that my depression is past, my readjustment complete. All I can say is that if you are also on a journey that is in any way similar to mine, from one place to another, or from one state to another, then give yourself time and trust that God will not leave you. I've told my story truthfully, with all my fears and worries, to encourage you on your journey. This verse that came to me at a dark moment last November has carried me into this year: 'Let him who walks in the dark, who has no light, trust in the name of the LORD and rely on his God' (Isa. 50:10).